Old Eyemouth and Burnmou
Lawson Wood

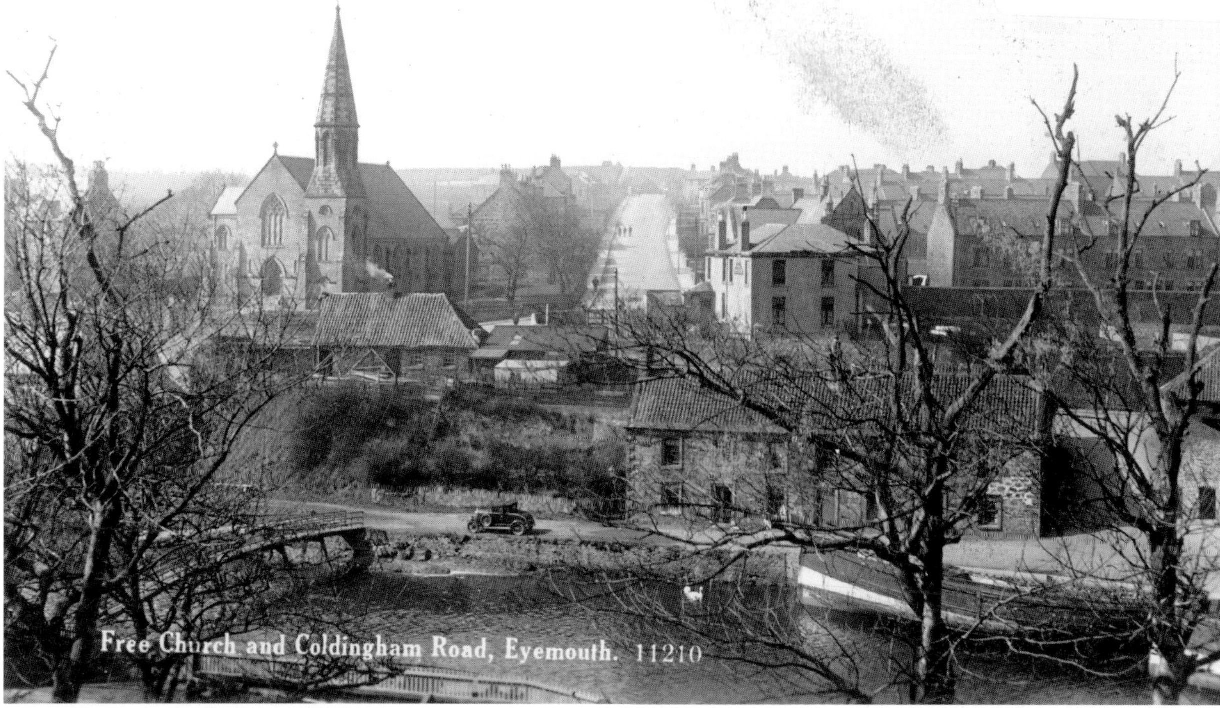

A view looking *"ower the witter"* from above Brown's Bank over the former home of the captain of the famous tea clipper *Cutty Sark* and up Coldingham Road. This wide new thoroughfare with its grand mansions intersected Victoria Road, Albert Road, Church Street and Harbour Road adjacent to where the former church manse and now Churches Hotel stands. The motor car dates the photograph to around the turn of the century, but it is difficult to tell what type of car this actually was. The old wooden bridge across the River Eye was swept away in the great flood of 14th August 1948 when the town was once again the scene of a great disaster, but no lives were lost at this time. The large church spire is that of the Parish church. As you can see, the location of the Catholic church was once a private home with smoke *"billowin oot its lum"*.

First published in the United Kingdom, 2010,
by Stenlake Publishing Ltd.
Telephone: 01290 551122
www.stenlake.co.uk

ISBN 9781840334890

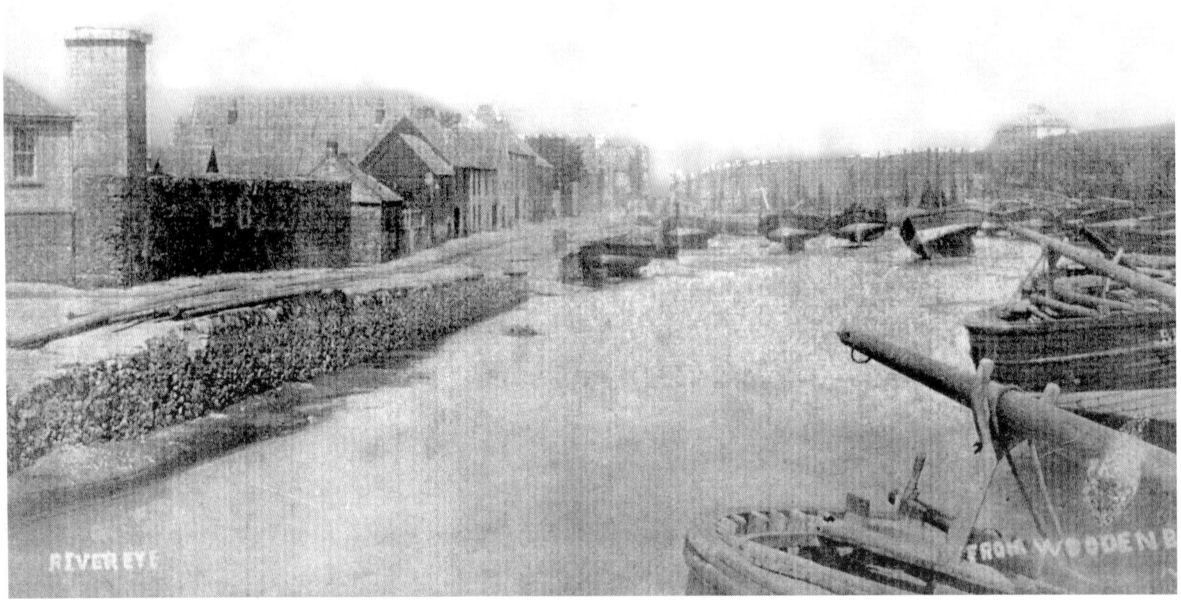

(Courtesy Eyemouth Museum Collection)

Whilst of very poor quality, the content of this photograph obtained through the Eyemouth Museum archives is important enough to include in this volume. It shows an early view of the present day harbour, but before the harbour was constructed and dredged. The river basin is beside what is now currently the FMA building and yard. It is low tide and the sail-powered fishing boats are all high and dry with their keels in the mud. The square tower to the left is the base of a former huge chimney, which was still standing, but the detail has been lost over time on this photograph.

Introduction

Linked by family, fortitude and fishing, the two coastal villages of Eyemouth and Burnmouth nestle in the far south eastern corner of Scotland. Almost touching the English border, these are the first or last two villages on the east coast of Scotland (depending on your direction of travel), both of which lie at the mouth of valleys with rivers which run into the sea. The River Eye terminates in a sheltered bay, with the village of Eyemouth wrapping itself around it, one of the only safe anchorages on the entire east coast. The Burn, really no more than a good source of fresh water for the old timers who once lived in the five separate villages at the foot of The Brae, ends at Burnmouth, two miles south of Eyemouth.

It is difficult to find early mention of Eyemouth, but when King Edgar of Scotland was dealing with the Benedictine Monks in Coldingham in 1098, the monks had secured 'two tofts' of land alongside the mouth of the river to facilitate the landing of their supplies and the selling or exchanging of produce with the locals. The first monastery was built at Coldingham in 837 by St. Aidan's monks from Lindisfarne and the first church in 1100. There are several old Roman roads in the region and the Ermine Way connects part of the road between Eyemouth and Coldingham, so it is only fair to assume that there was a settlement of some sort at the mouth of the River Eye, as the 'Roadsteads' as they are known, are the only sheltered safe haven for ships between Amble and the Forth. We do know that the bay was used as a staging post on the route north to the Antonine Wall and indeed, the old barracks at the northern end of the bay were said to have been of Roman origin, with the newer building built on the Roman foundations, as several artefacts were found during the excavation of the site and dated to the time of the Roman occupation.

Emuth as she was originally known had such a prominent position that she played a vital role in the peace of Europe. Her fortress, which guarded Eyemouth Bay, was deemed so important to the peace that the Treaty of Bolougne stated that Eyemouth Fort had to be utterly destroyed and never to be built again. In 1597 the new King James IV visited the town and declared Eyemouth a burgh of Barony with the added privilege of a free port. Now, no longer under the control of Coldingham Priory, the town enjoyed a very fruitful future of free trade and soon grew on the wealth of the smuggling between France and Scotland. There was said to be more wine drunk in Scotland at that time than ale. The old town area around the harbour with its trademark narrow wynds and vennels was perfectly suited for the smuggling enterprise which was centred around the imposing Gunsgreen House with its underground cellars, vaults and secret passageways. It was said that at the turn of the eighteenth century there was more of Eyemouth underground than above. During new construction in the old town, the builders always come across ancient passageways and vaults which have to be made secure. In the mid-eightenth century it was noted that Gunsgreen also had a very profitable distillery: *yielding about 1500 gallons of aqua weekly, chiefly derived from potatoes, 6000 cwt. of which have sometimes been consumed in two months*. This is rather bewildering to say the least, as we all regard 'Aqua' as water, but with the processing of 6000 cwt or 300 tons of potatoes every two months (for the production of raw potato alcohol or a primitive vodka), then we have figures that show 300 tons of potatoes distilling 12,000 gallons of alcohol every two months! Now Gunsgreen House has been completely restored to its original glory and her massive vaults are open to the public. There was also a whisky distillery at Brown's Bank.

Both villages at the mouth of a fresh water resource are linked by two distinct events, the first being the impetus for the second. The first catastrophic event occurred in October 1881. On that morning, the sea was like a millpond, 'wi' barely a ripple', but the weather barometer was falling drastically. Nevertheless, virtually the entire east coast fishing fleet set out to sea on the outgoing tide that morning as usual. That day the entire east coast was hit by a massive and sudden cyclone, the likes of which had never been known before. Acknowledged as the worst Scottish fishing disaster ever recorded, it is known as The Great Storm of October 1881. Locally, in Eyemouth it became known as 'Black Friday.' After weeks of bad weather the local fleet were becoming impatient to go to sea. On Friday 14th October 1881, they awoke to a calm morning. Ignoring the low readings on their barometers, they put to sea. By midday they had just begun their line fishing when the whole country was hit by a violent storm. The boats rushed home but many failed to make it safely into the harbour. They either capsized or smashed on the Hurkar Rocks at the harbour entrance. Their families on the pier looked on helplessly. That day, the east coast fishing fleet lost 189 men: 129 from Eyemouth, 24 from Burnmouth, fifteen from Newhaven, eleven from Cove, seven from Musselburgh, and three from Coldingham Shore (St. Abbs). 93 widows and 267 children were left weeping on the shore as they watched the boats being dashed to pieces in front of their eyes (figures from Rev. McIver's book).

As a direct result of the loss of so many men, an extension to the Great North Railway was approved and a branch line was opened to Eyemouth, as there simply were not the men left in the town to transport the fish by horse and cart up to the main line railway station at Burnmouth. Construction of the Eyemouth Railway Station and branch line started in 1885 and opened for business on April 13th 1891, almost ten years after the 'Disaster'.

Burnmouth on the other hand is not quite as old, but stems back from the Flemish immigrants into the area. Originally from the Dutch and Belgian lowlands, they were expelled from England by Henry II around 1183. Burnmouth was actually five distinctly separate villages. The village at the top of the hill was called Flemington (the old Flemington Inn burned down in mysterious circumstances just a few years ago). At the bottom of the hill were the hamlets of Partanhall, Lower Burnmouth, Cowdrait and Ross. Ross now only comprises of four houses and is located furthest south along the coastline near to Ross Point headland. Ross was deemed an entirely separate village as it was located outside the parish boundaries of Ayton and located in the Parish of Mordington. There was once an ancient mill situated in the gorge, but no sign of this can be found now. With a fresh supply of spring water at the bottom of the gorge and a sheltered basin for ships, the village 'Doon the Brae' soon developed independently and her first harbour was built in the 1830s at a cost of £1,600 with three quarters being defrayed and paid by the Fisheries Commissioners and £400 being paid by the local fishermen. The harbour was further extended in 1879 at a cost of £9,000 with a beacon placed at the end of the outer breakwater and again in 1959 when the old works were restored.

During the 1800s and first half of the last century the main industry undertaken by the fishermen was inshore fishing for lobsters and edible crabs, known locally as 'poos'. Interestingly, the name Partanhall comes from the partan or shore crab, which was once collected as bait for the long line fishermen. On the day of the great storm, 24 men who had set sail from Burnmouth were lost from five local fishing boats. Women, children and old men looked on from the shore as the frail boats were dashed against the rocks as they struggled to gain the safety of the harbour. The ships lost were the *Excellent; Christina; Alice; Transcendent* and the *Guiding Star*.

Burnmouth has always had its roots in the sea and the shore line. Whilst men worked on the fishing boats, groups of women worked in the herring industry, gutting the fish as soon as they arrived in Burnmouth Harbour. Speed was of the essence to gut and salt the fish before they went soft. Kelp was also manufactured with the raw material collected from the shore, but the return was never enough for the locals to earn enough of a living from it. Periwinkles were also collected and were soon an item of export from the village, for the use of those fishmongers who converted them into sauce.

The East Coast Main Line passes along the top of the cliff and Burnmouth's railway station opened in 1846 and finally closed, along with all of the local stations in 1962. Thousands of barrels of cured herring were transported from the harbour by large ship or by taking the catch up the hill on horse and cart to load it into goods wagons in the sidings at Burnmouth Station. Boats with larger catches would wait for the tide at Eyemouth and land the herring there.

Lawson Wood, St.Abbs, 2009

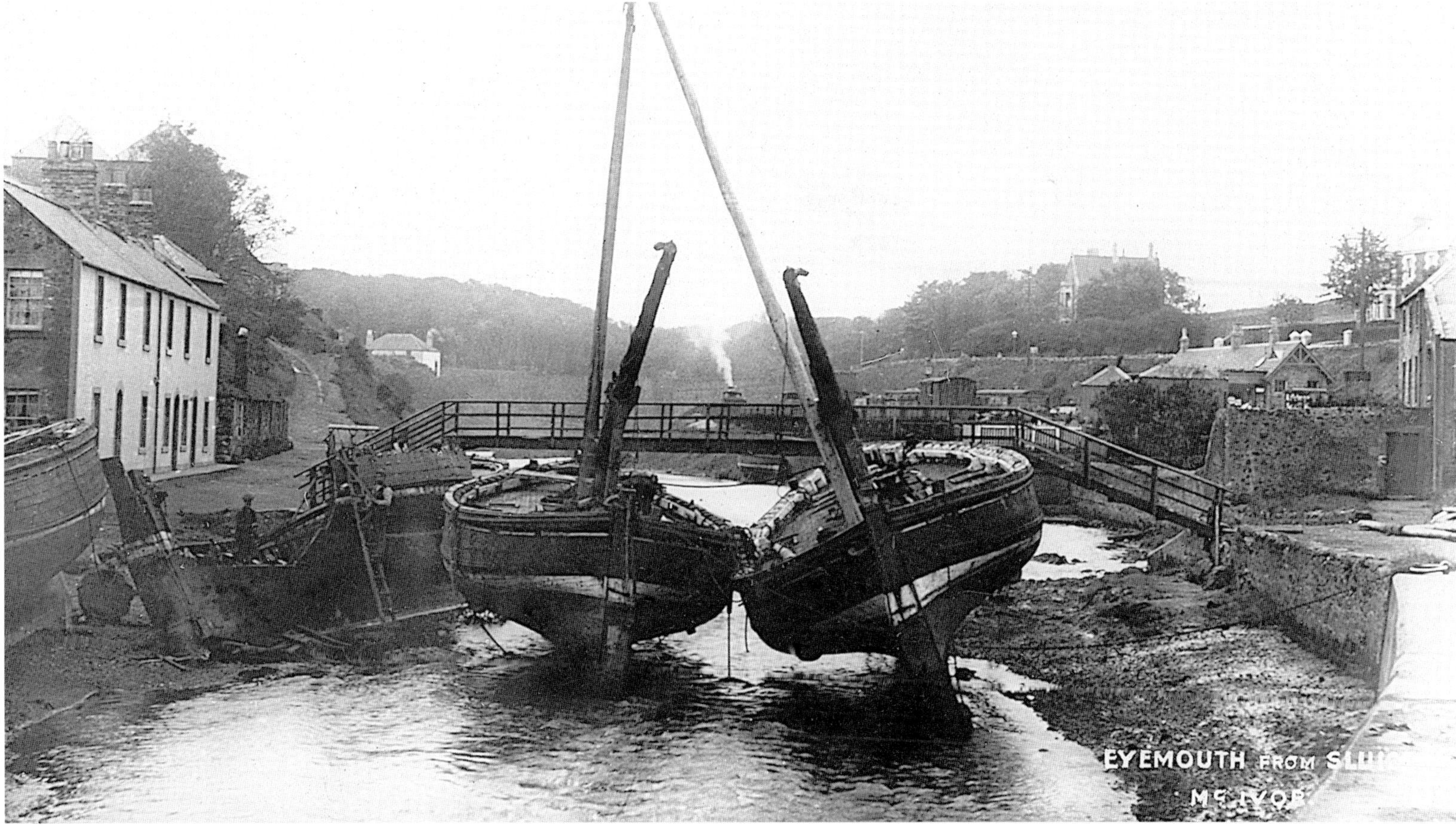

Some time after 1891, but not by too many years, this view looks up the River Eye, virtually blocked by two sail-powered fishing yawls. Note that they both have closed-in decks and are anchored next to J.Weatherhead's boatyard who originated this new and radical design for the Scottish fishing fleets. To the left is Brown's Bank, once a former whisky distillery, now the shipyard's offices and stores. To the right a train is running off a full blast of steam and smoke before it starts its journey back up to the main line railway station at Burnmouth. The branch line was predominantly used for transporting fish up to the main line and thence on to the commercial markets in Leith or London. Due to the steep gradient of the line, fish offal and water would always run out onto the tracks creating a dangerous situation during the winter months, whenever it was freezing, as this would make the railway tracks slick with ice; there were several instances when the trains failed to stop and crashed into the barriers in the station. At the top far left of the photograph can be seen the old toll house. The bridge over the river is still called the Toll Bridge to this day.

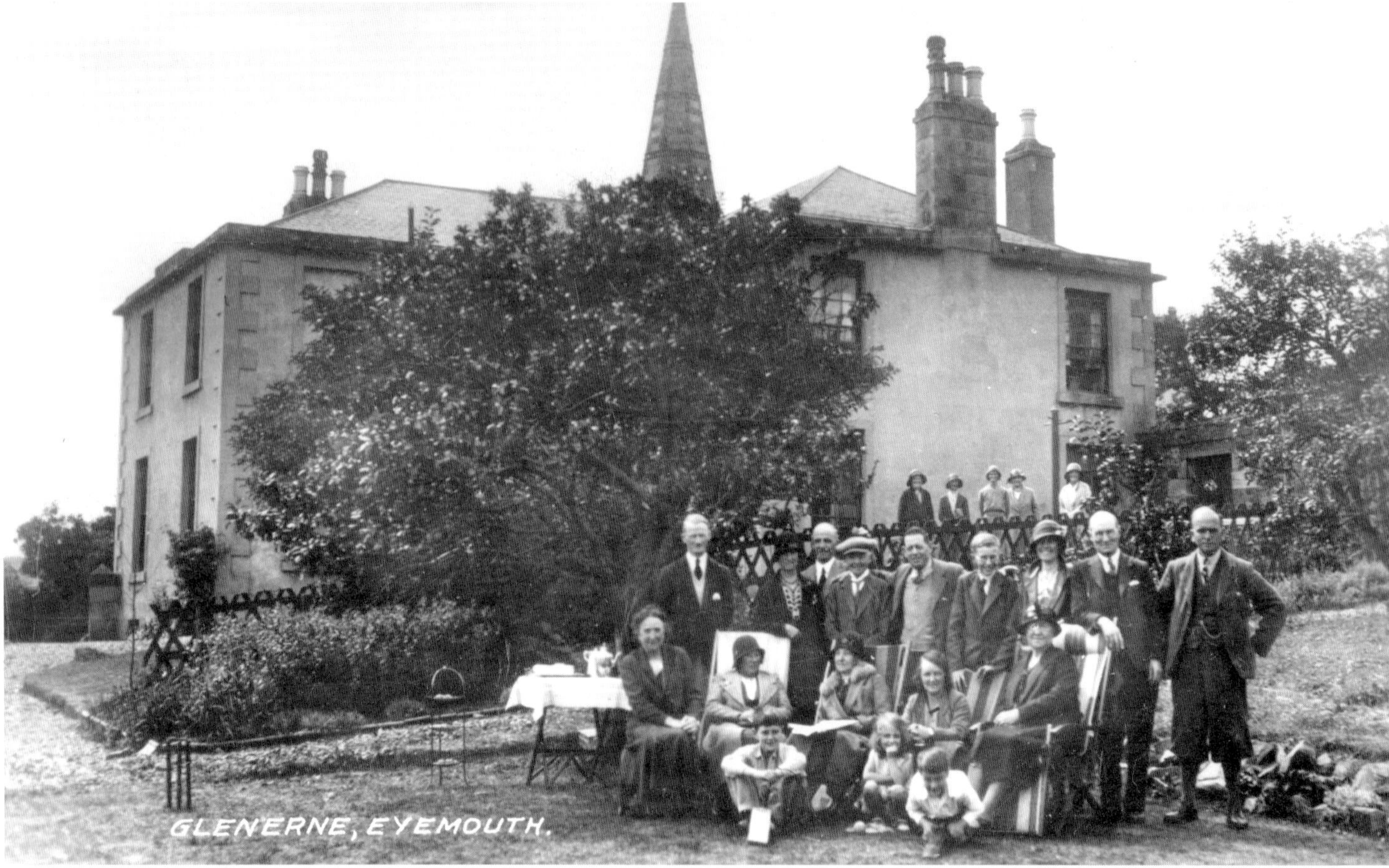

This property was built around 1790 before any other mansions were constructed along Victoria Road. It later became the manse of the Free Kirk which was once used as the local cinema. The Former old church on Church St. was finally demolished and apartments built on the site. Afterwards this house became a private house again and guest house alternatively over many years, eventually it became the Glenerne Hotel which was popular with guests. This since underwent a huge tansformation in 2000 and it is now known as Churches Hotel (what else could you call a hotel situated on the 'Holy Corner' of Eyemouth).

This scene is taken in the 1920s/1930s judging by the clothes. This large group of guests and probably the owner's family are outside having tea whilst the youngsters had been playing cricket on the lawn.

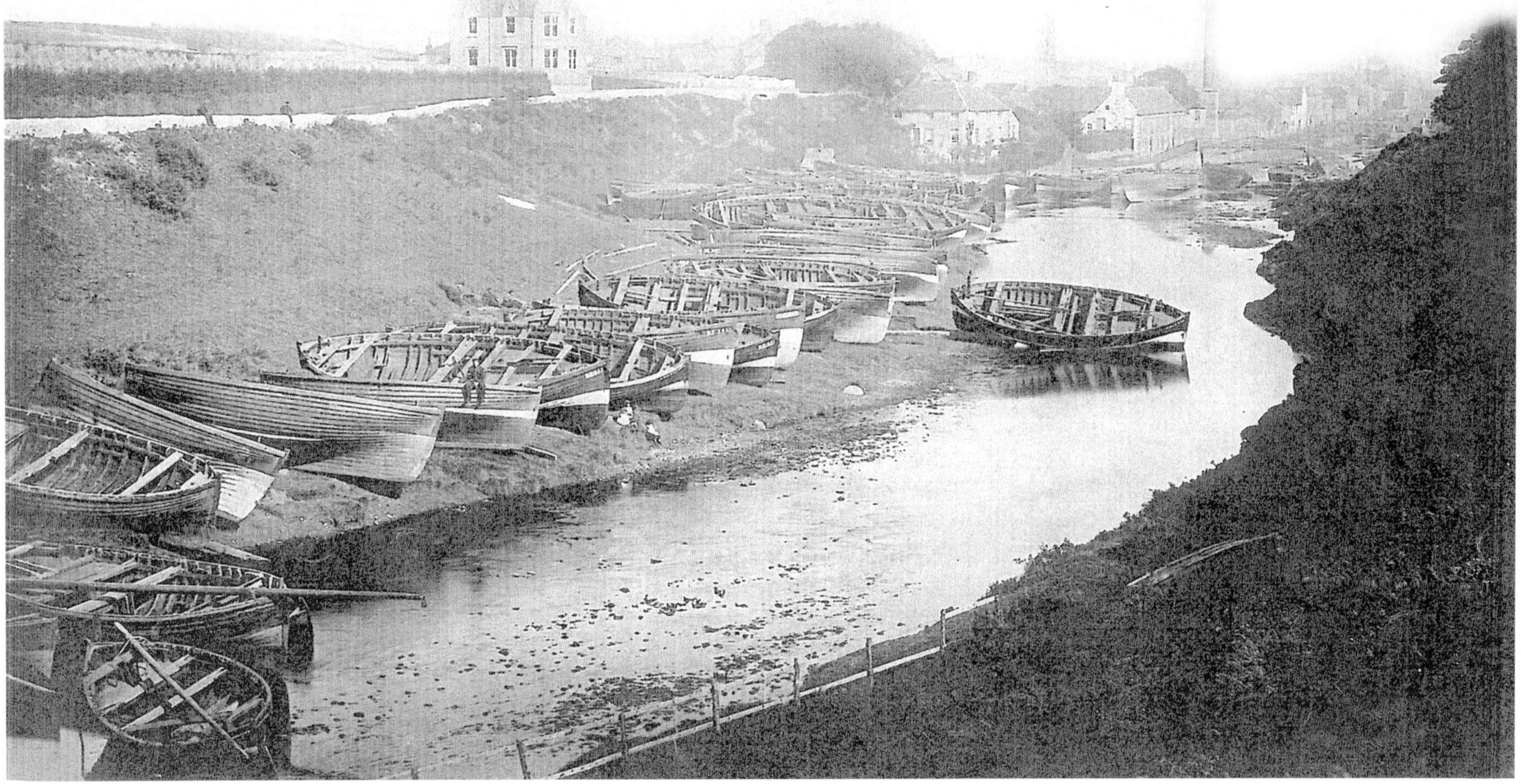

The summer fishing boats were rowed up the river at high tide and pulled onto the river bank with the aid of round 'roller' logs. Considering that this view dates before the Eyemouth railway was built in this location, or indeed that there is only the one house on present day Victoria Road, this is a remarkable vignette of the fishermen's lives, probably taken around the time of the Disaster in 1881 and certainly before 1885, as it took six years before the railway station opened for service. Note that all of the summer boats had open decks to accommodate the rowing fishermen and all of their nets and lines. The boatbuilding company of J. Weatherhead were the pioneers of closed in decks and Eyemouth fishing vessels were the first to have them.

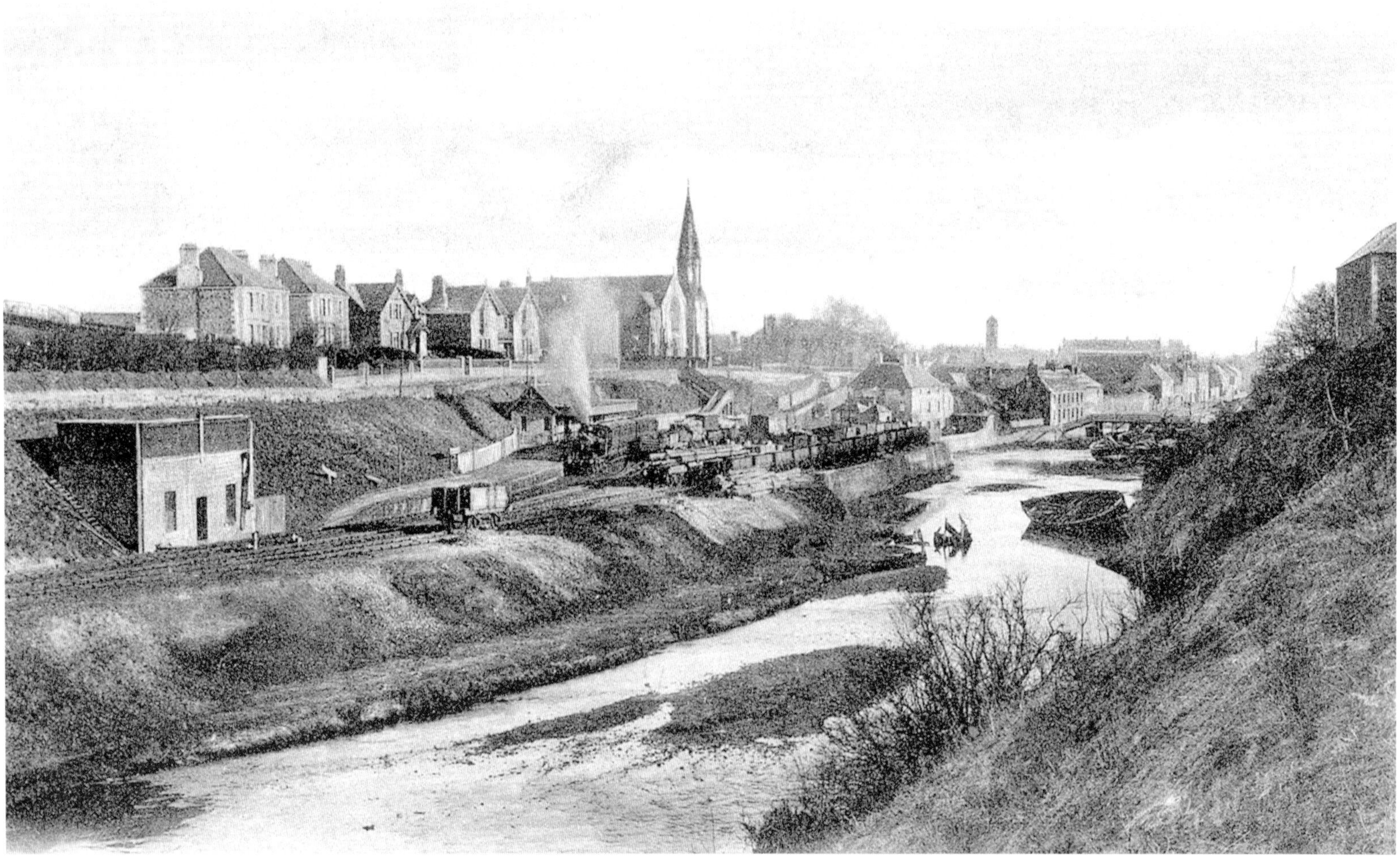

Now, it is after 1891 and the railway line has been constructed. The river bank has been shored up and filled in to make a new level area for the termination of the Eyemouth Branch Line and the large private houses are gradually extending along Victoria Road above the railway station. Blowing off a full head of steam, this train is getting ready to leave Eyemouth Station to travel up to the main line link at Burnmouth, a journey that would take only 8 ½ minutes, the shortest commercial train journey of any railway line in the British Isles.

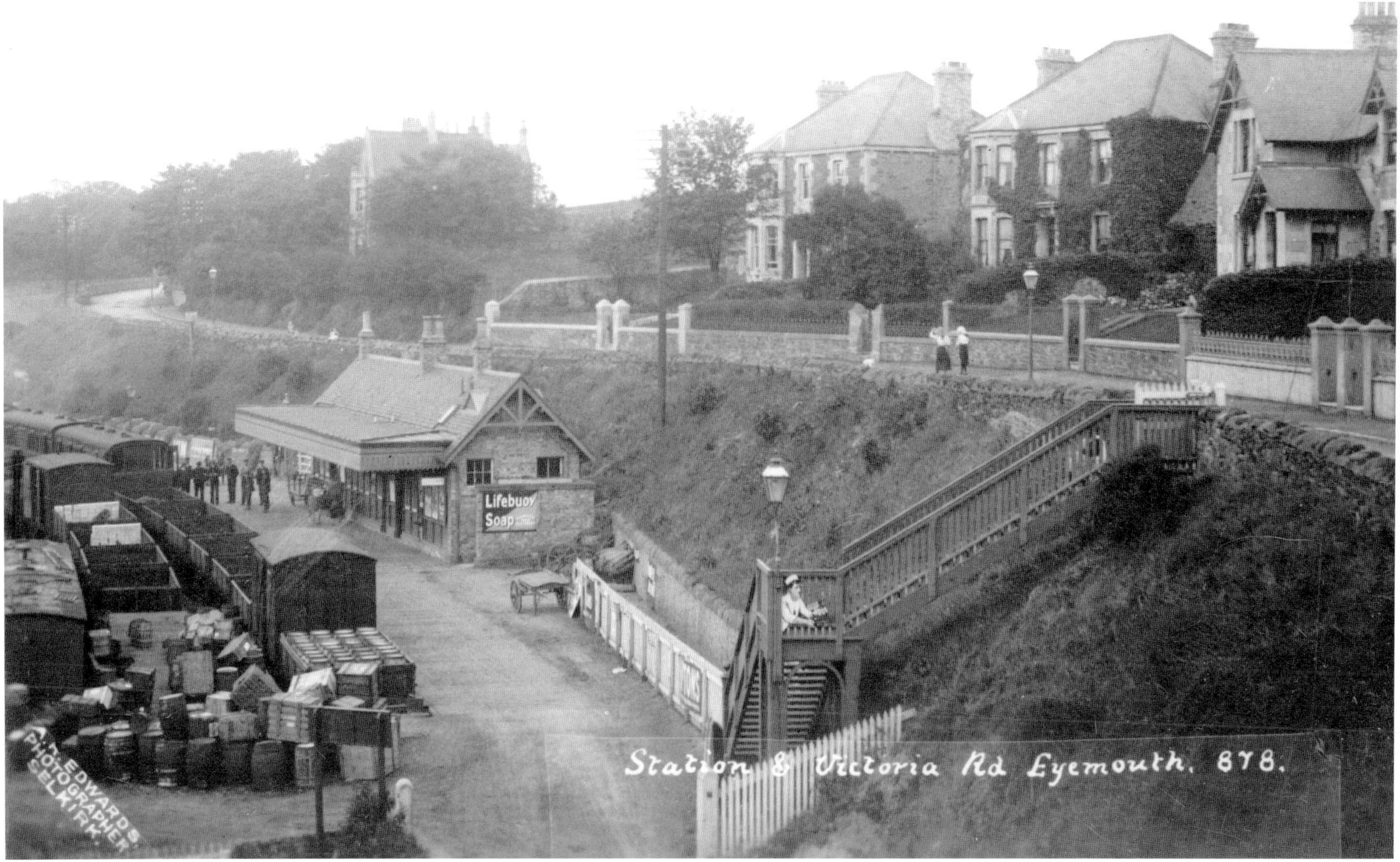

Construction of Eyemouth Railway Station and the branch line started in 1885 and it opened for business on April 13th 1891, almost ten years after the 'Disaster'. Undoubtedly the railway not only saved the town, it revitalised the fishing industry, further prompting much-needed improvements to the existing harbour facilities and also started a new and strange phenomenon in this small coastal village – tourism. The superb sheltered bay and golden sandy beach was a lure for the Victorians who came in their droves to sample the 'healing waters' of the North Sea. This era saw the start of the bed and breakfast establishments and the forerunner of what is now Churches Hotel opened for business as it was directly opposite the exit from the railway terminus.

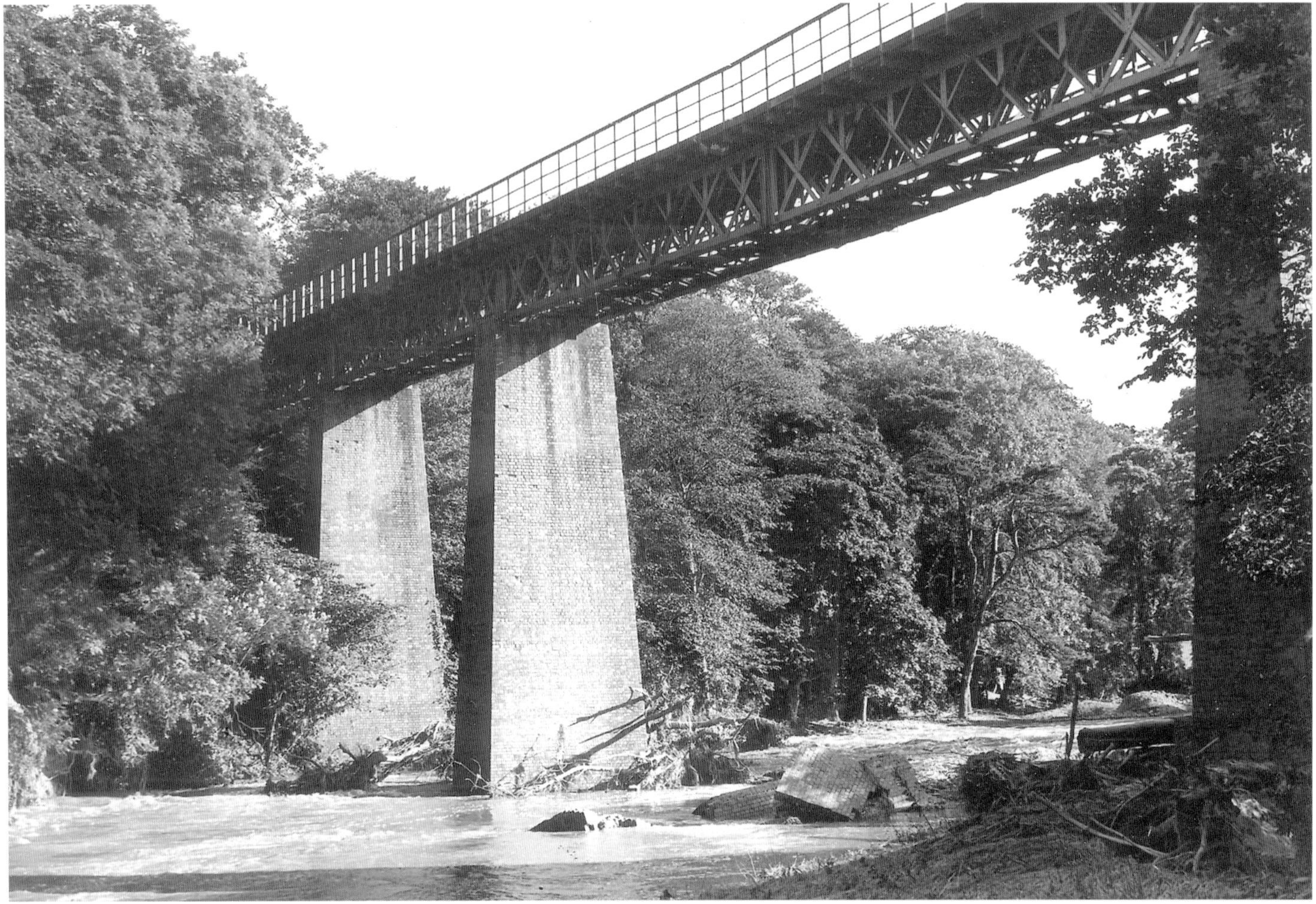

However much those healing waters improved the spirits of the visitors the town's spirits were severely dampened in August of 1948 when a massive storm ravaged the countryside. So much rain fell in such a short space of time that virtually all of the main line railway bridges were washed away and a culvert on the main embankment next to the River Eye collapsed, trapping millions of gallons of water behind the rapidly eroding embankment. The bridge over the River Eye lost its central pier and whilst the railway line did not collapse, it put the Eight Minute Link out of action for months and months, virtually ending the tourism boom and plunging Eyemouth into another realm of despair, unseen for many years.

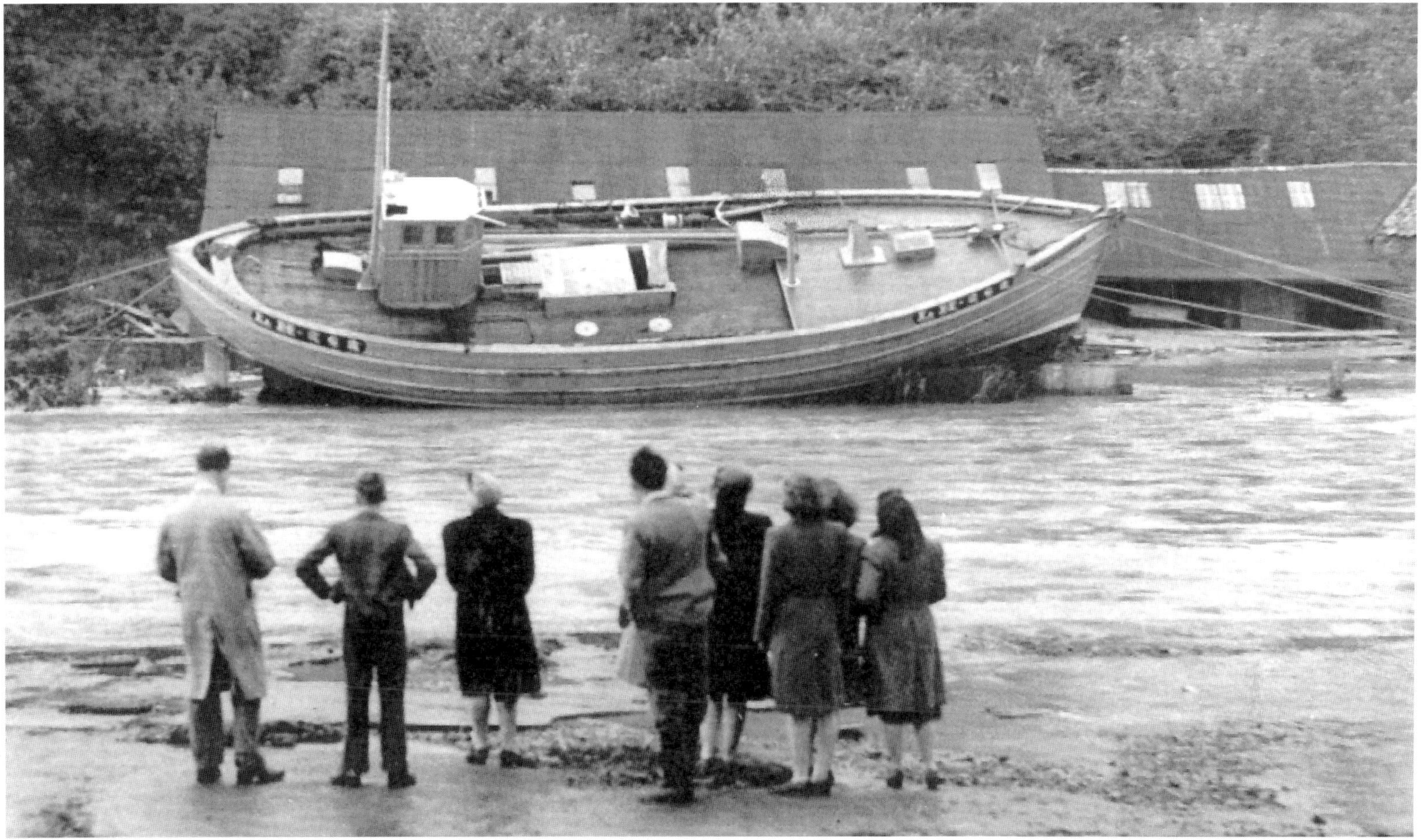

(Courtesy Margaret Squires Collection)

All of the rivers from East Lothian down into Northumberland and west into the heart of the Scottish Borders broke their banks and in some areas entire villages were flooded. Millions of acres of crops were destroyed and thousands of farm animals drowned. The River Eye at Eyemouth was no exception. In the midst of the chaos, should the trapped water have broken through, Eyemouth would have been wiped out by a tidal wave of proportions unheard of. The River Eye was already bursting its banks and a newly-launched fishing boat from J.Weatherhead's boatyard was actually put back on its stocks (albeit rather crookedly).

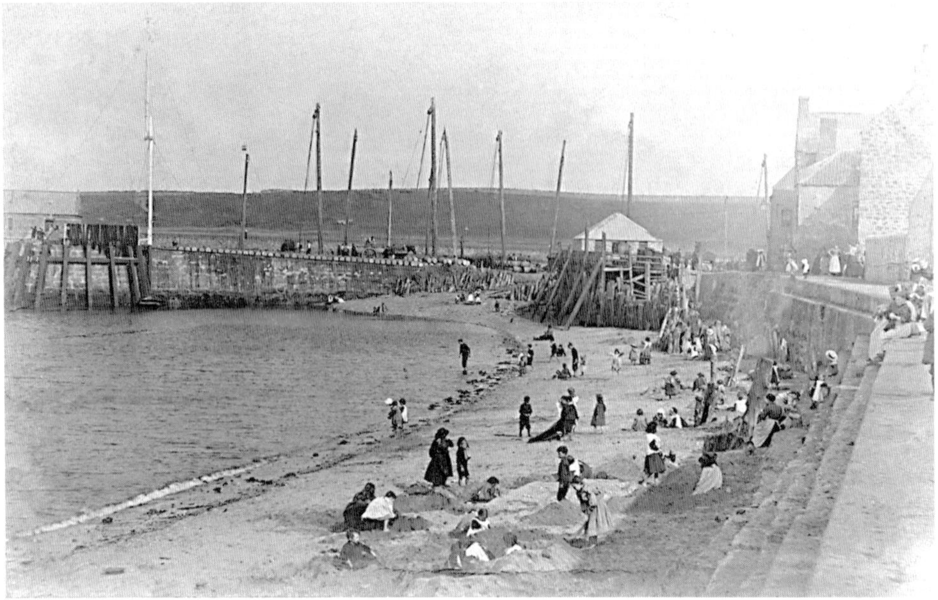

Whilst this photograph has been published elsewhere, it is worthy of inclusion in this volume due to the age and interest value of this pleasant beach scene, photographed at the turn of the last century. There was no sea wall in this section, just large and rough concrete steps to stall the ferocity of the waves. The tide is advancing slowly, gradually overtaking all of the Victorian children's sand castles and the late afternoon sun is casting a shadow onto the beach. The old Cobble House is now built, but quite clearly there is urgent repair work needed to that end of the bay as the wooden supports and pilings are desperately in need of repair, as is the slipway onto the beach. The old styled pierhead has a number of hemp ropes and lines hanging out to dry and rows of barrels lie waiting to be filled with salt herring. Several fishing boats masts can be seen in the background and judging by the dress the people on the beach are wearing, this photograph would have been taken sometime over the weekend.

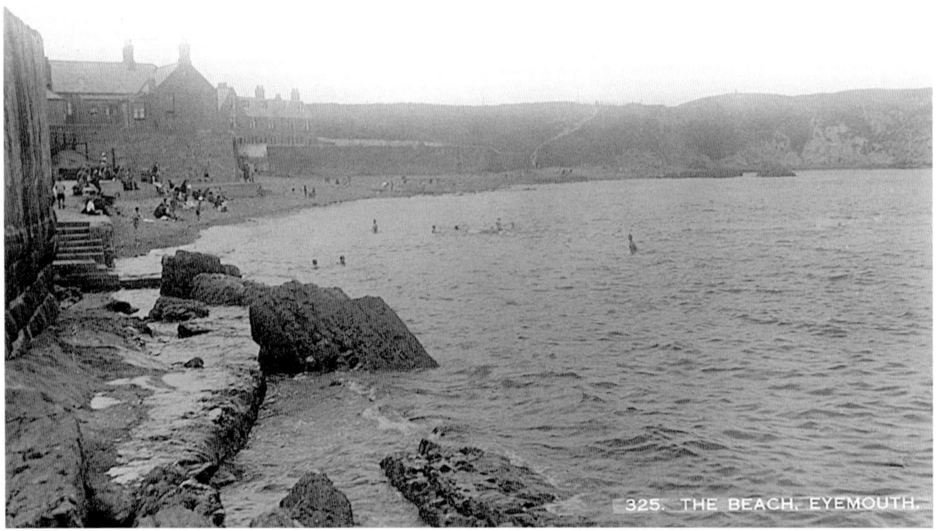

This postcard is a bit of a misnomer, as it advertises Eyemouth Beach, when clearly at this state of tide, there is very little beach left at all and the old tumble-down sea wall is in virtual ruins. The photograph had to have been taken in the summer as there are people bathing. This was taken long before Eyemouth Caravan Park was first built by the Wood family.

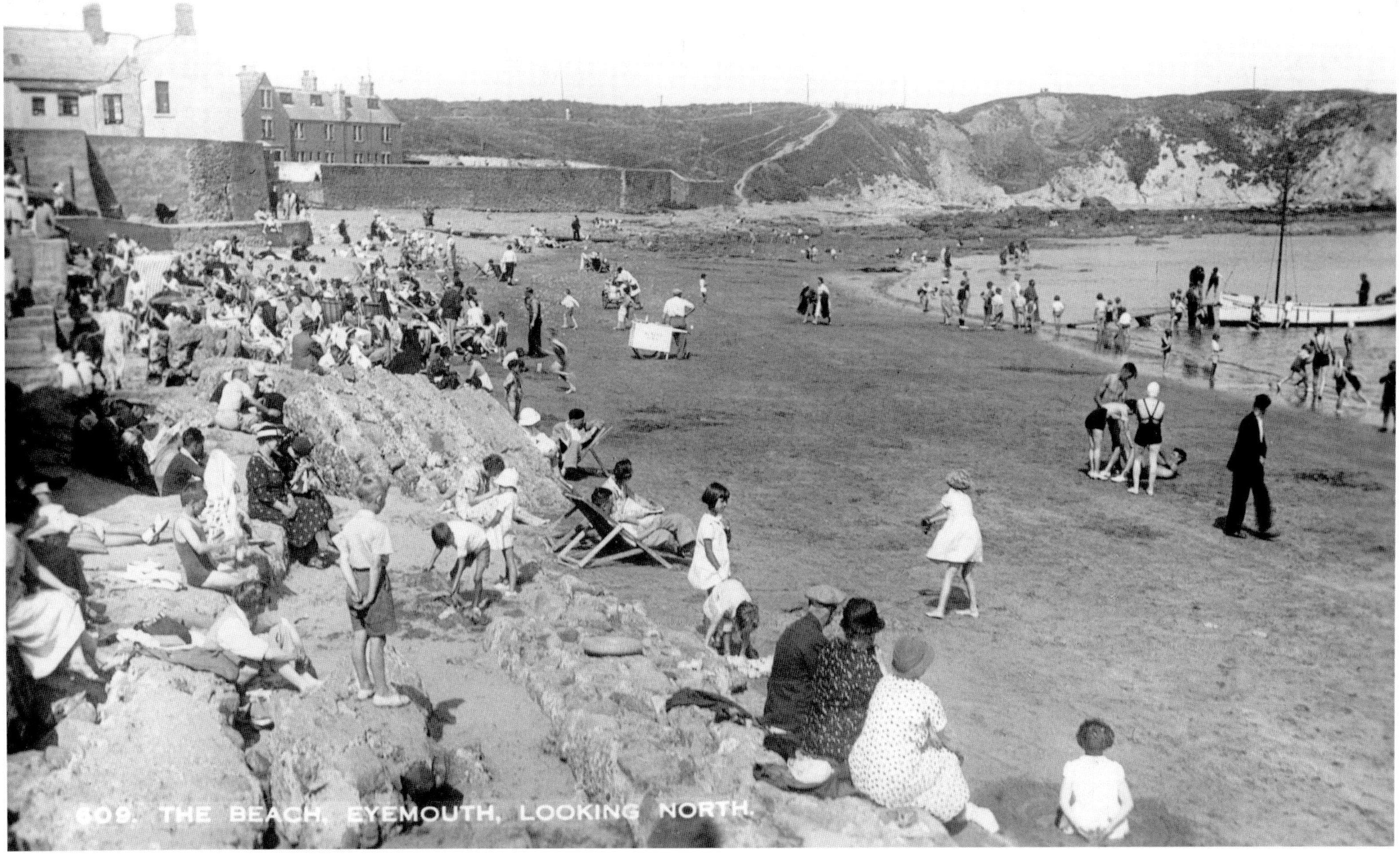

Same view or very close to it, but with a rising and falling tide of over 6 metres or twenty feet, Eyemouth Bay loses its beach twice each day, but when the tide does go out, there is a huge expanse which can fit all the tourists who visit the coast. At this time there were deckchair rentals, ice cream vendors on the beach, floating diving and swimming platforms, and stepped pontoons to gain access to small craft for trips around the bay. Still no caravans up on the top of North burn and still a crumbling old sea wall which would not be replaced until 1949. The caravan park did not start until around the same time, the Wood family having bought Northburn Farm from David Gray in 1945.

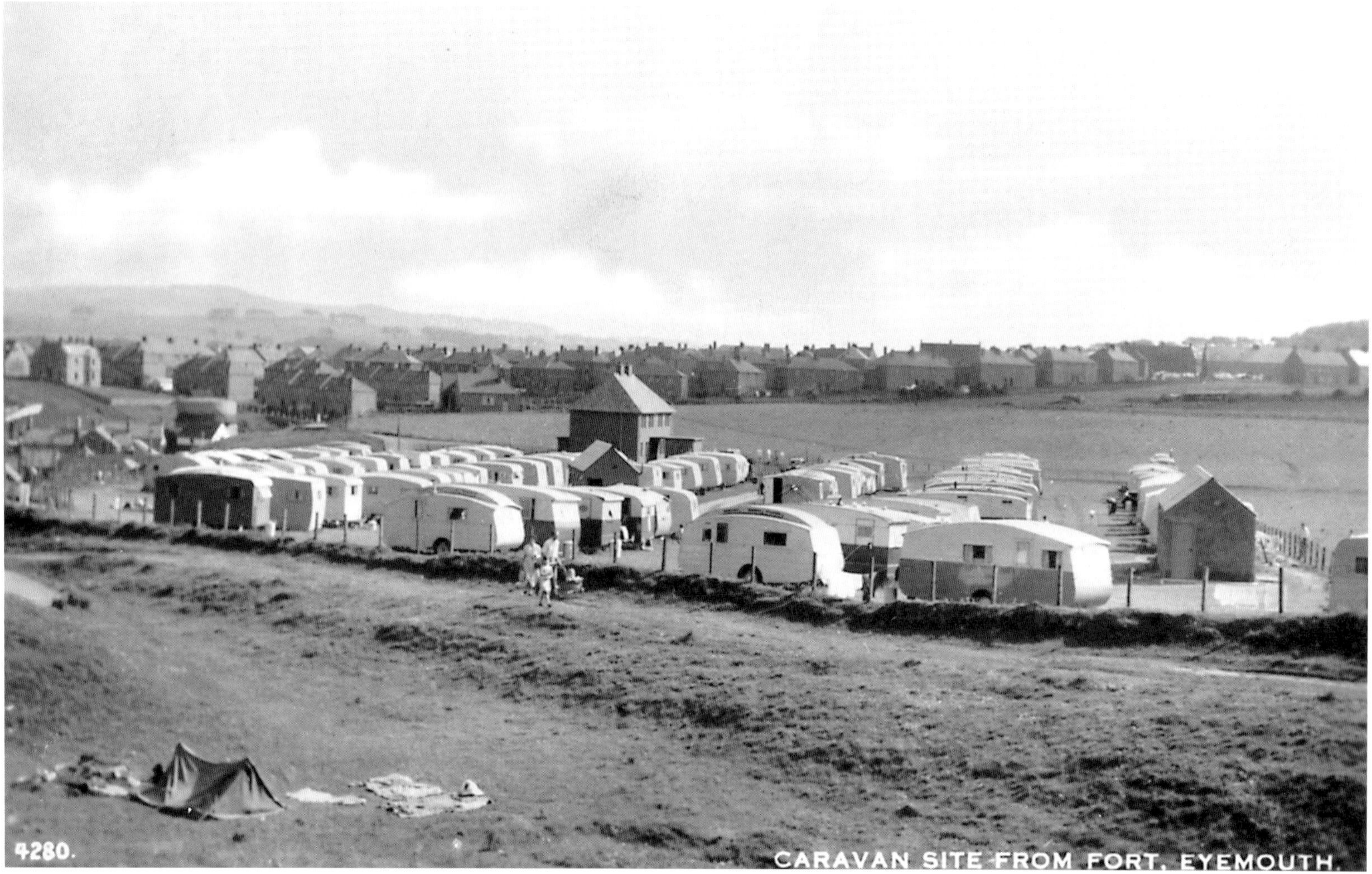

Robert and Barbara Wood who had bought Northburn Farm started a holiday caravan park in the town which undoubtedly helped the economy of all the businesses for over 55 years under the same ownership. Needless to say that the design of the more modern holiday caravans has radically changed over the years. These older style caravans were fitted with gas lamps and cookers, coal fires and absolutely no electricity, fridges, television or any of the modern conveniences expected as standard in the very latest models.

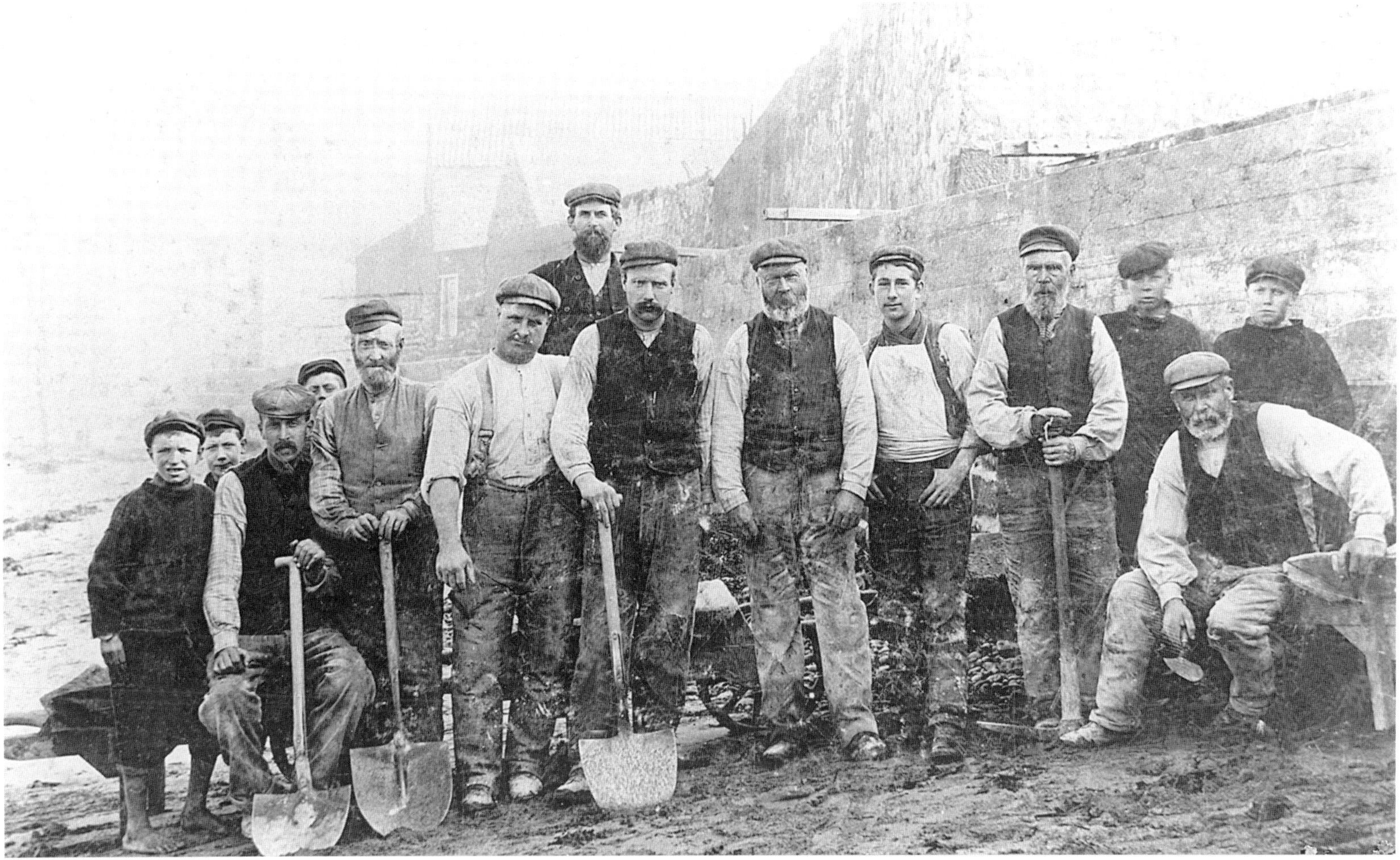

(Courtesy Eyemouth Museum Collection)

Building the first breakwater was an arduous task, as the interior of the bay was made of sand and shingle with bedrock only to be found at the northern end of the bay where the North Burn terminated in the sea near to the old coastguard houses and army barracks and stables. The work was entirely dependent on tides and weather. The sea had to be calm, as there would be a very real danger otherwise of it undoing all of the workmen's hard labour. The relentless pounding of the North Sea finally took its toll and undid all of the year's work. A new promenade, or the 'bantry' as it is called, was built in 1949.

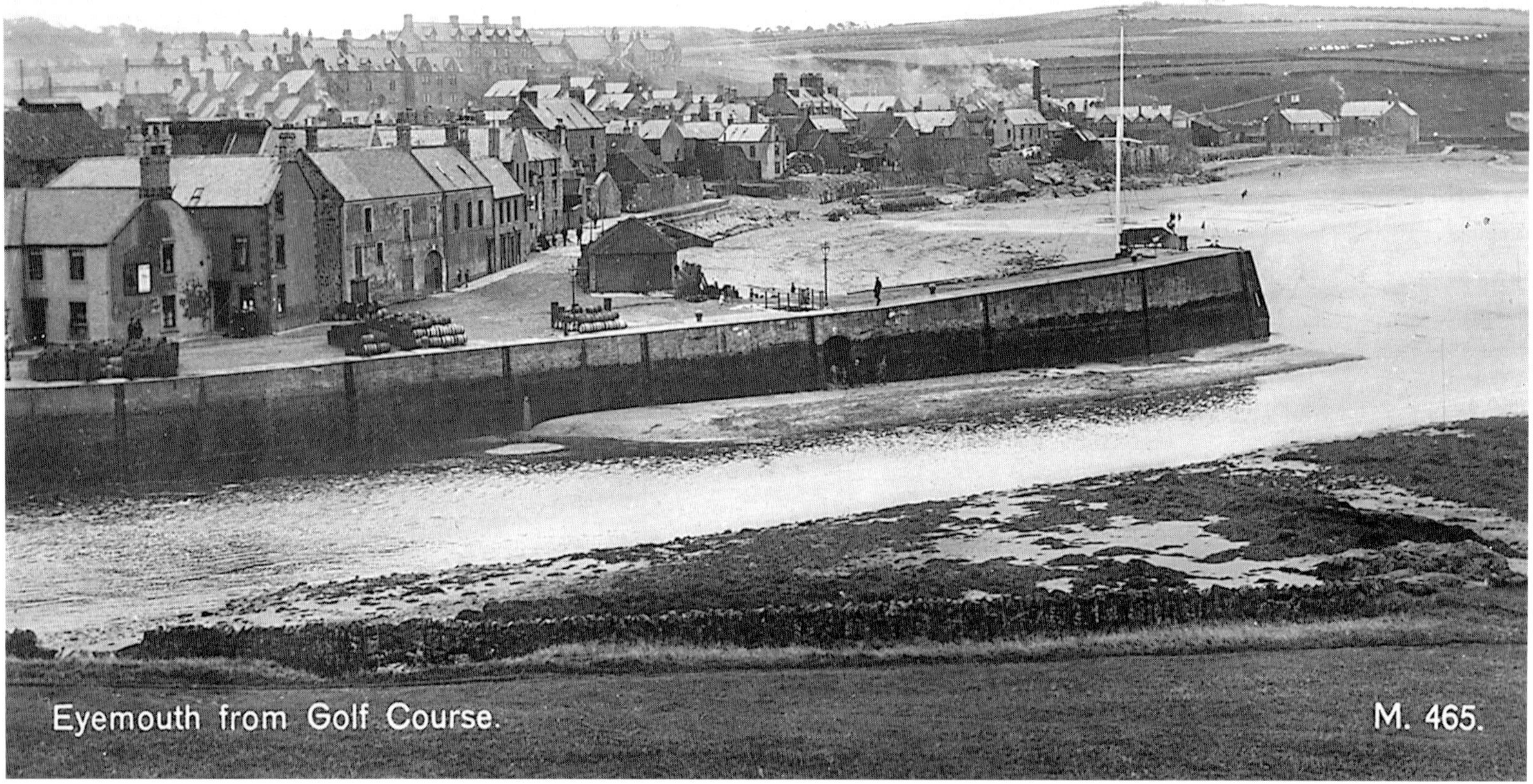

A view proclaiming to be photographed from the golf course, not quite accurate, but the golf course is one of the oldest in Scotland. However this highlights one of the main difficulties of the old harbour at the mouth of the River Eye, which still causes problems, and that is of the silting up of the harbour. This view shows the small sandbar which has collected at the bottom of the stairs. There was an entryway down from the harbour quayside in front of the old cobble house to allow access to the fishing boats which used to tie up there. The old stairs were always slimy and rather disgusting in appearance and smell! In the background you can clearly see how badly the concrete breakwater has broken down with huge sections of wall lying on the beach. The gasworks chimney is belching smoke and the pier is littered with stacks of herring barrels. This first pier and pier head was built in 1750 at a cost of £2,000, the cost of which was raised by subscription.

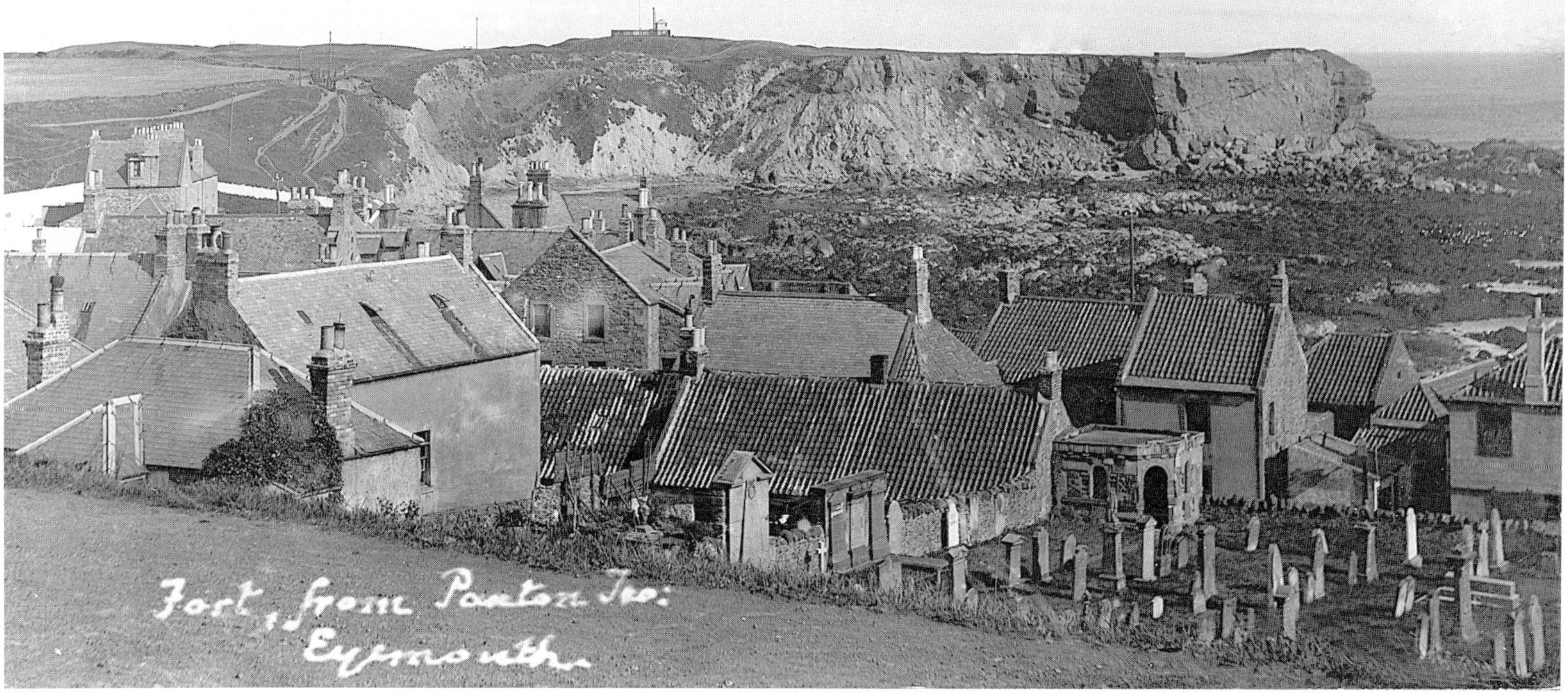

At the opposite end of the bay and the view of the Fort Point taken from the hill above the old cemetery. This view is completely changed and has been for a number of years. The old coastguard lookout station up on the hill has since been demolished, the ammunitions bunker near the edge of the cliff has very little left of it, several paths lead up to the Cliffside, but now there are no caravans at the cliff edge. The graveyard is full (in fact it was so full at one time that an extra layer of soil was put in to accommodate victims of a smallpox epidemic). All of the buildings have been demolished in front of the graveyard and now replaced with a wonderfully attractive car park and amusement arcade.

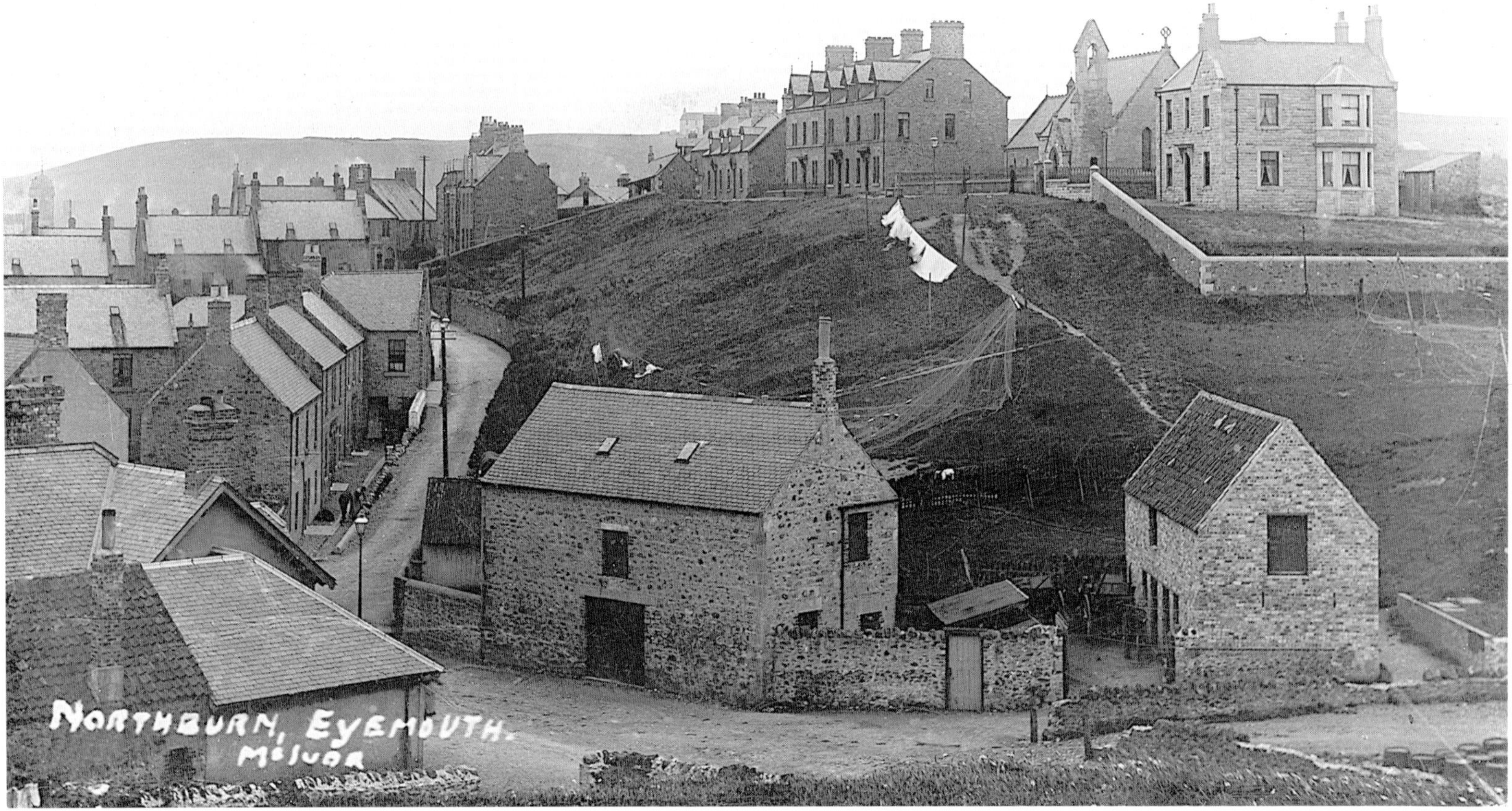

Northburn, of course is named after the North Burn which runs down the main road and is detoured underground down North Street and into the sea at the northern side of Eyemouth Beach. At the bottom of Northburn Road, the buildings of Northburn Farm are still located at the left of the photograph, but the buildings in the foreground at the bottom of the hill are long gone. This former church was converted into a garage, but was then torn down and a new garage was built in its place with a forecourt and petrol station. A huge unsightly gas tank was installed on the road up Hurkar Road, now since gone too. The green hillside was used for drying the washing and fishing nets.

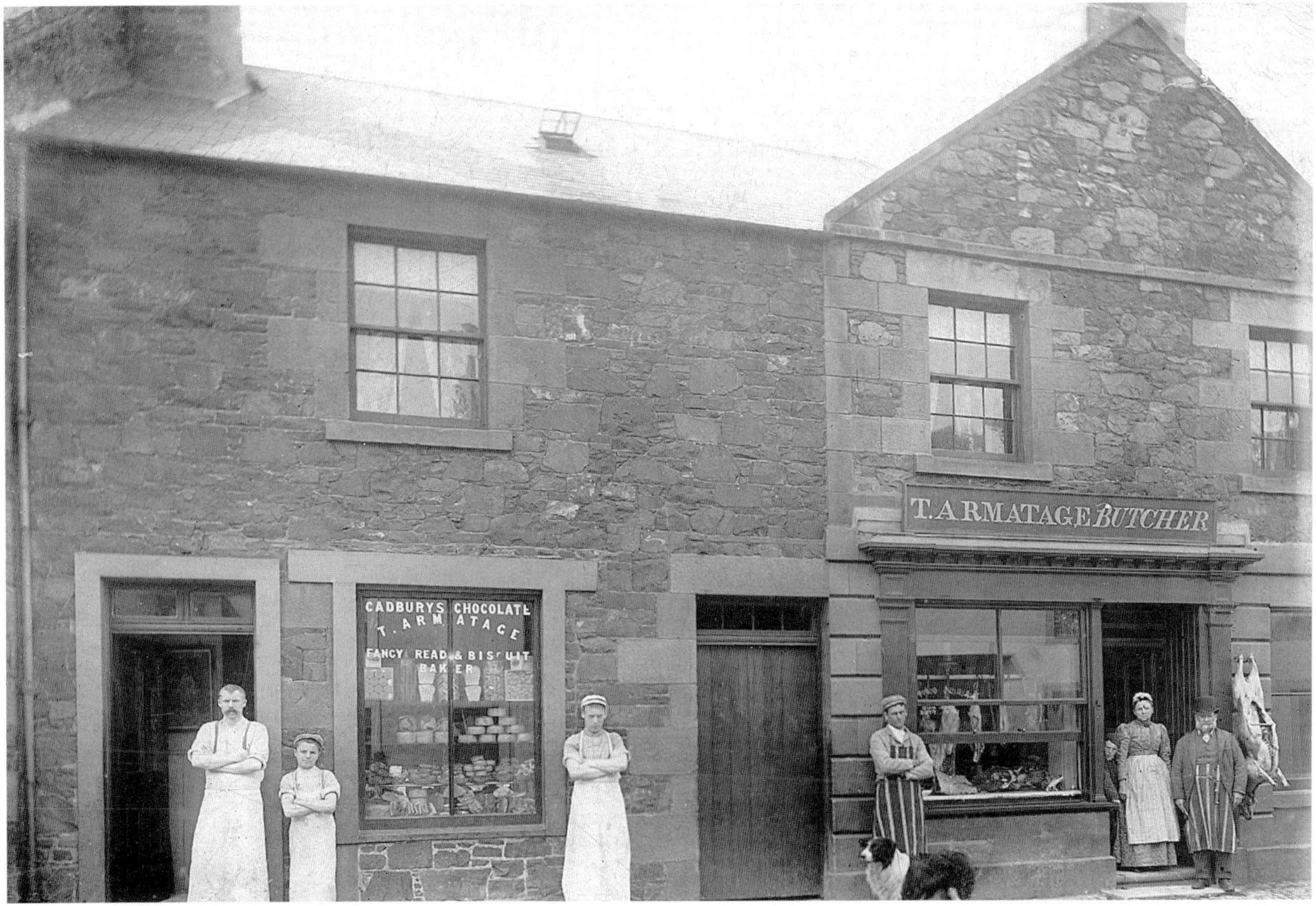

In the Market Square, Armatage the Butchers & Bakers were a well-established business and principally served the townsfolk of Eyemouth. All of the surrounding little villages had their own butchers and bakers and tended to keep the business to themselves. However Mr. Armatage also had a horse and cart and latterly a charabanc from which he collected and purveyed his goods to a wider audience. Hardly a scene to inspire Environmental Health, here we can see the butcher's shop window open to allow patrons to handle the meat they were buying and a whole pig is hung outside the shop. This shop remained a butchers until only a few years ago when the business of David Walker was sold to make way for a Chinese takeaway. My grandfather, William Dougal, owned and operated another butcher's business just to the left of the bakery division of Thomas Armatage and operated the butchery business for many years. This butcher's shop is now a baker's. Incidentally the street adjacent to Thomas Armatage's butchery business is called Armatage Street.

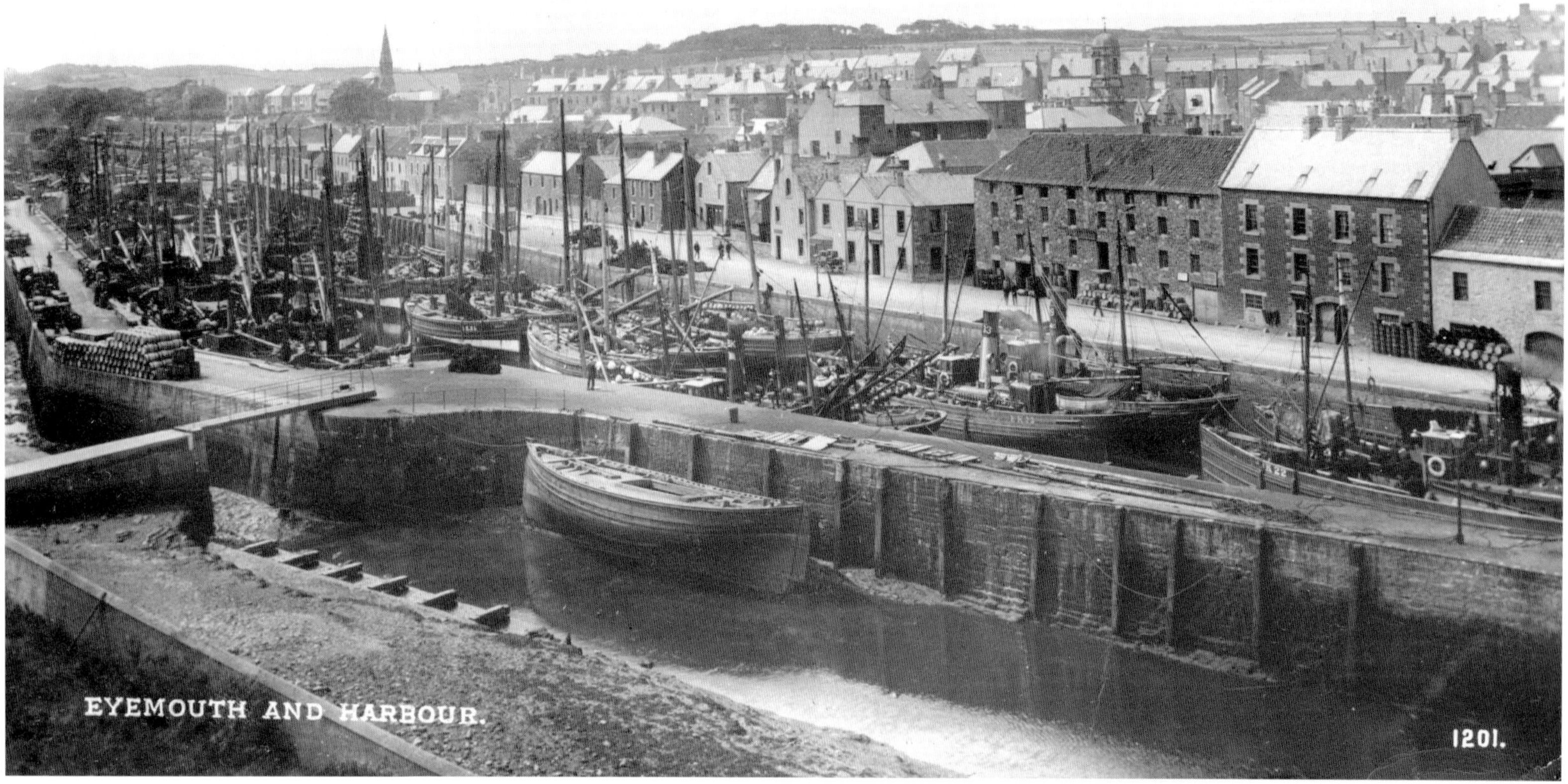

It is difficult to imagine the changes that have been undertaken in and around Eyemouth Harbour and quayside over the last hundred years or so. From having no moorings or deepwater basin and being entirely reliant on the state of the tide and the river, to having long quays on both sides of the harbour, the erection and subsequent decline of two fishmarket buildings, the radical change in the use of the harbourside buildings and of course the fishing fleet, now so seriously depleted that the habour has had to diversify its use to visiting yachts, scuba diving businesses and a maritime museum. Between 1809 and 1820 an average production of 10,000 barrels of herring a year were processed in Eyemouth with over 150 boats assembled to set sail to the inner fishing grounds.

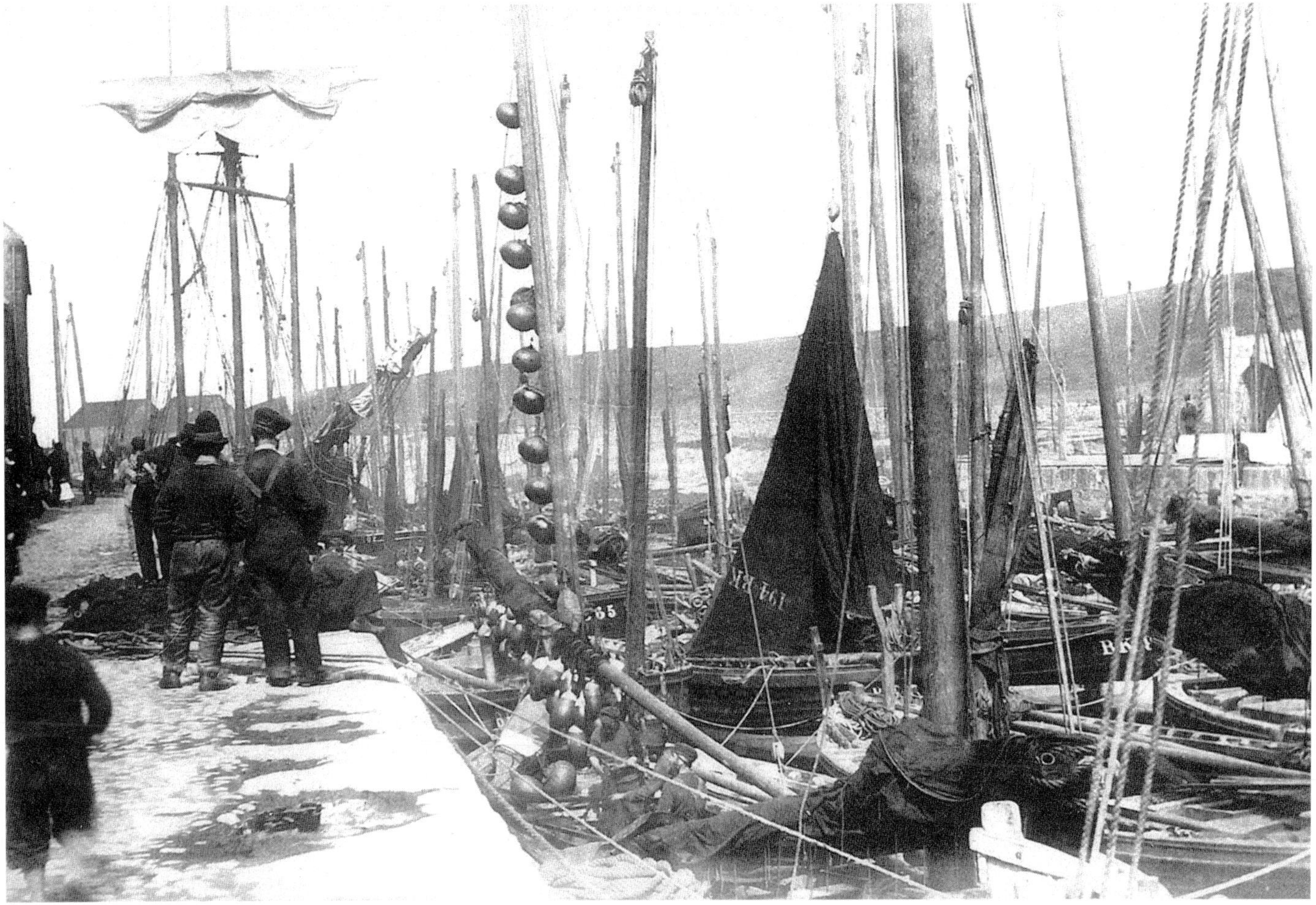

Sitting opposite the old Whale Inn lies part of the herring fleet, the quay is loaded with nets and ropes and the ox/pig bladder floats are hanging up the mast to dry. The main sail of the fishing boat in the centre is being strung up upside down. The old archway to the underground cellars of Gunsgreen House is visible. What is of great interest is in the background of the photograph. You can clearly see the huge masts of a three-masted schooner or Barquentine with her cross spar's sail hanging down. This ship would be in Eyemouth to carry the barrels of cured herring to the markets of Russia, Germany, Poland and the Caribbean. Of further interest are the two buildings which look like they are situated on the other side of the harbour, but before the old lifeboat shed was built. What they were, who lived in them or what they were used for is a mystery.

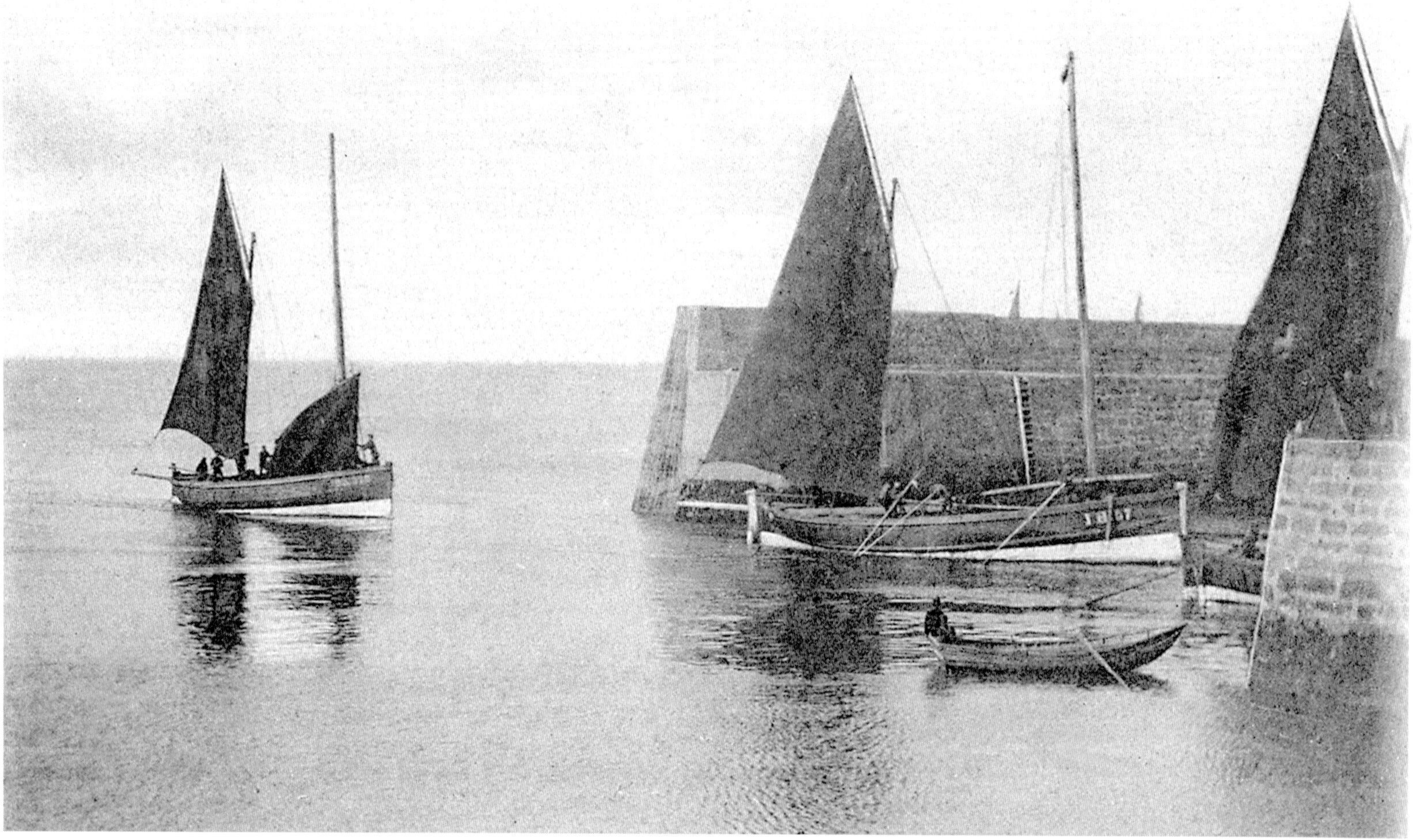

At the turn of the tide, the boat boys quickly dropped the lead sail and with usually a crew of seven men, six would work the oars with the last steering as they gained entry into the heavily silted harbour. The narrow entrance and breakwaters were designed and built by John Smeaton (whose lighthouse still stands on Plymouth Hoe) and built with rock from the old fortifications overlooking the bay in 1770. Smeaton said *The harbour of Eyemouth lies in a corner of the bay, in which ships can work in and out at all times of the tide, or lie at anchor secure from all winds, except the northerly or north-easterly*. A 'callant' is sitting in one of the punts just in case any of the fishing fleet founders on the sand bar and needs help to unload the fish and get it ready for market.

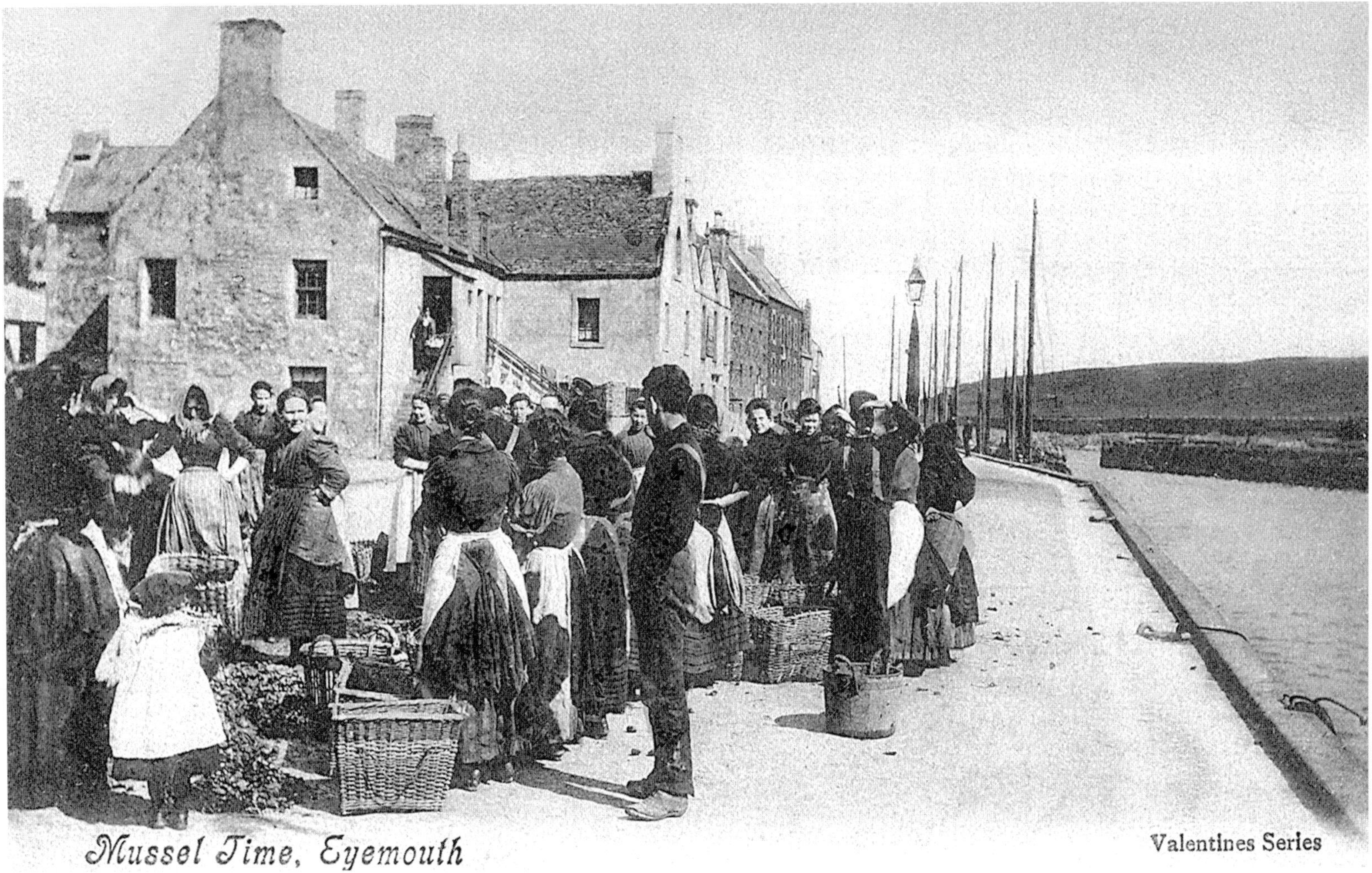

This fine vignette of working life proudly advertises 'Mussel Time' on Eyemouth quayside. Usually the family of a fisherman would bait the lines with freshly picked mussels. But here a large group of women have gathered around an enormous pile of mussels to bait the lines for several of the boats. Some of the long-lines would have as many as three hundred hooks per line and these would be used predominantly to catch cod and mackerel. The baited hooks were placed on 'lintries' (line trays) with grass between the hooks to stop them hooking on each other.

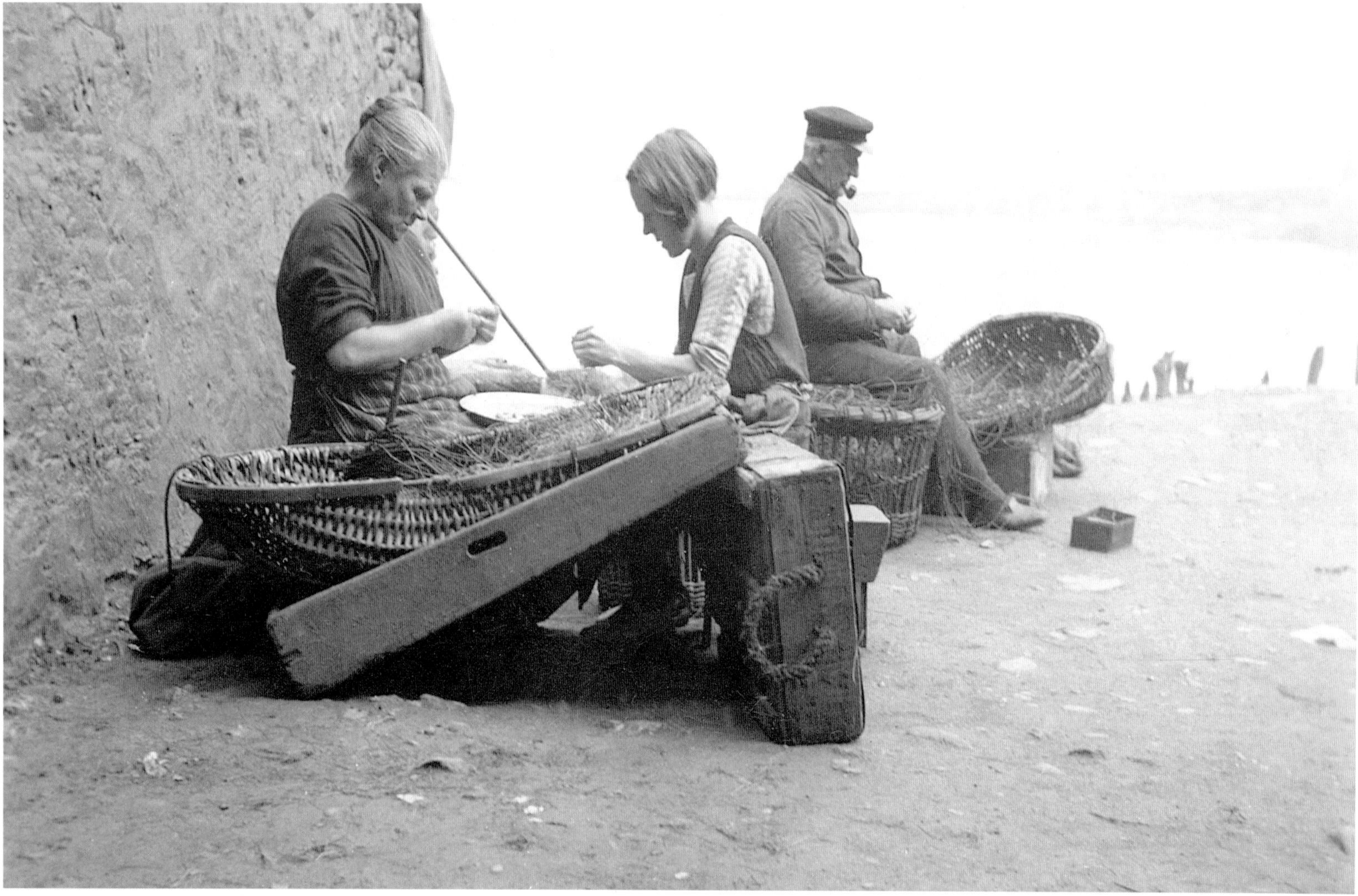

Undoubtedly the baiting of the hooks for the long-line fishing was one of the most important jobs of the day. There would be literally thousands of hooks to be baited with mussels or limpets each day. Each hook was separated by a tuft of grass to stop them snagging as they were stored into the lintries (line trays). This fisherman and his wife are sitting at the end of the old pier head with the Hurkar rocks in the background.

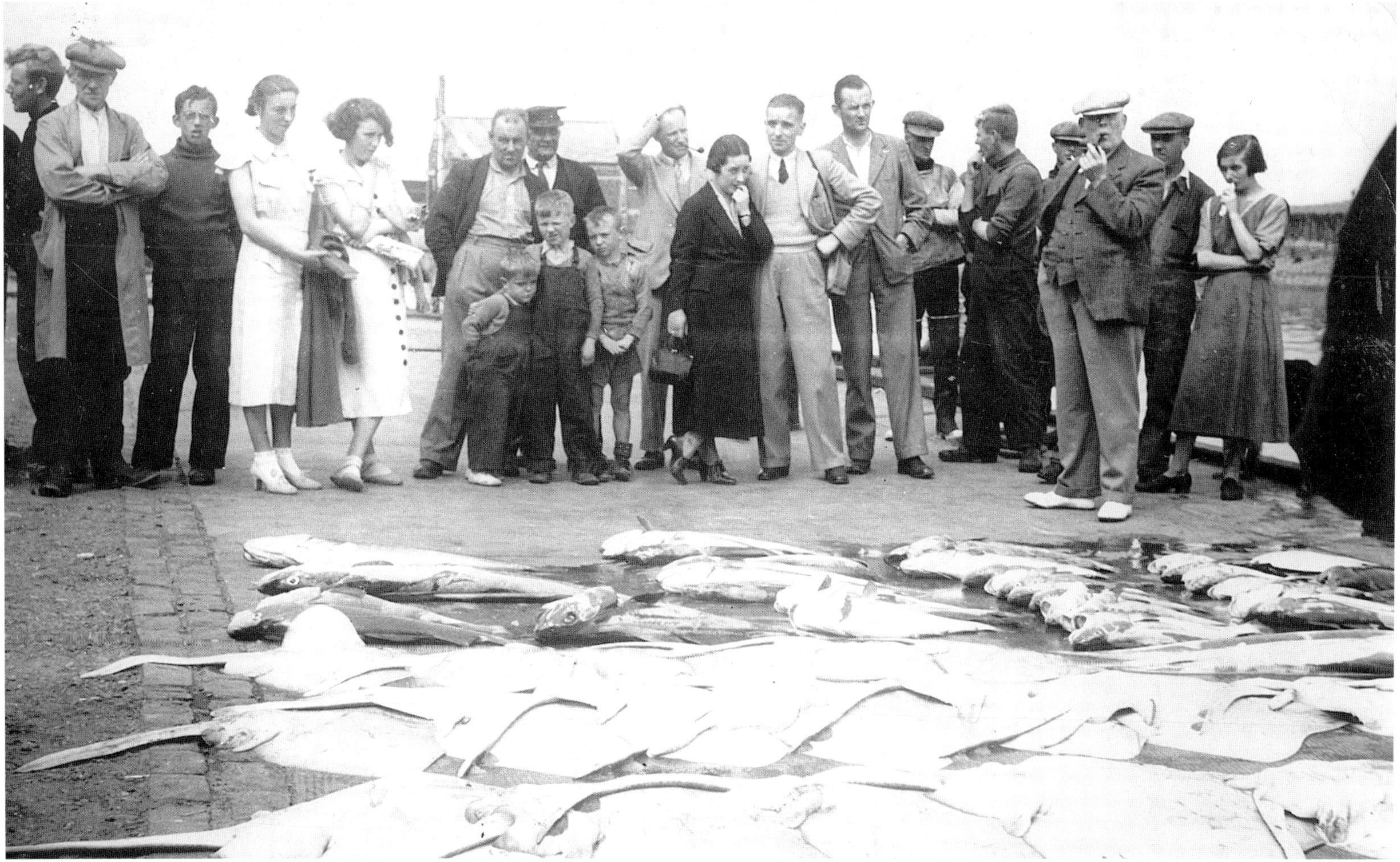

After the fish were landed, the catch from each boat was spread out over the harbour road and the crowds gathered each day to here the banter of the local auctioneer as his 'gobbledegook' somehow managed to be understood by the fishermen and their agents as individual fish were sold. Here a catch of skate, turbot, halibut and cod are on view to the general populace. Hardly health conscious, the market was eventually moved indoors to a private audience of fish 'cadgers'. Even that has stopped now, as much of the catch is already sold before it even reaches shore and is offloaded directly onto waiting, refrigerated, articulated lorries, without ever having gone to market.

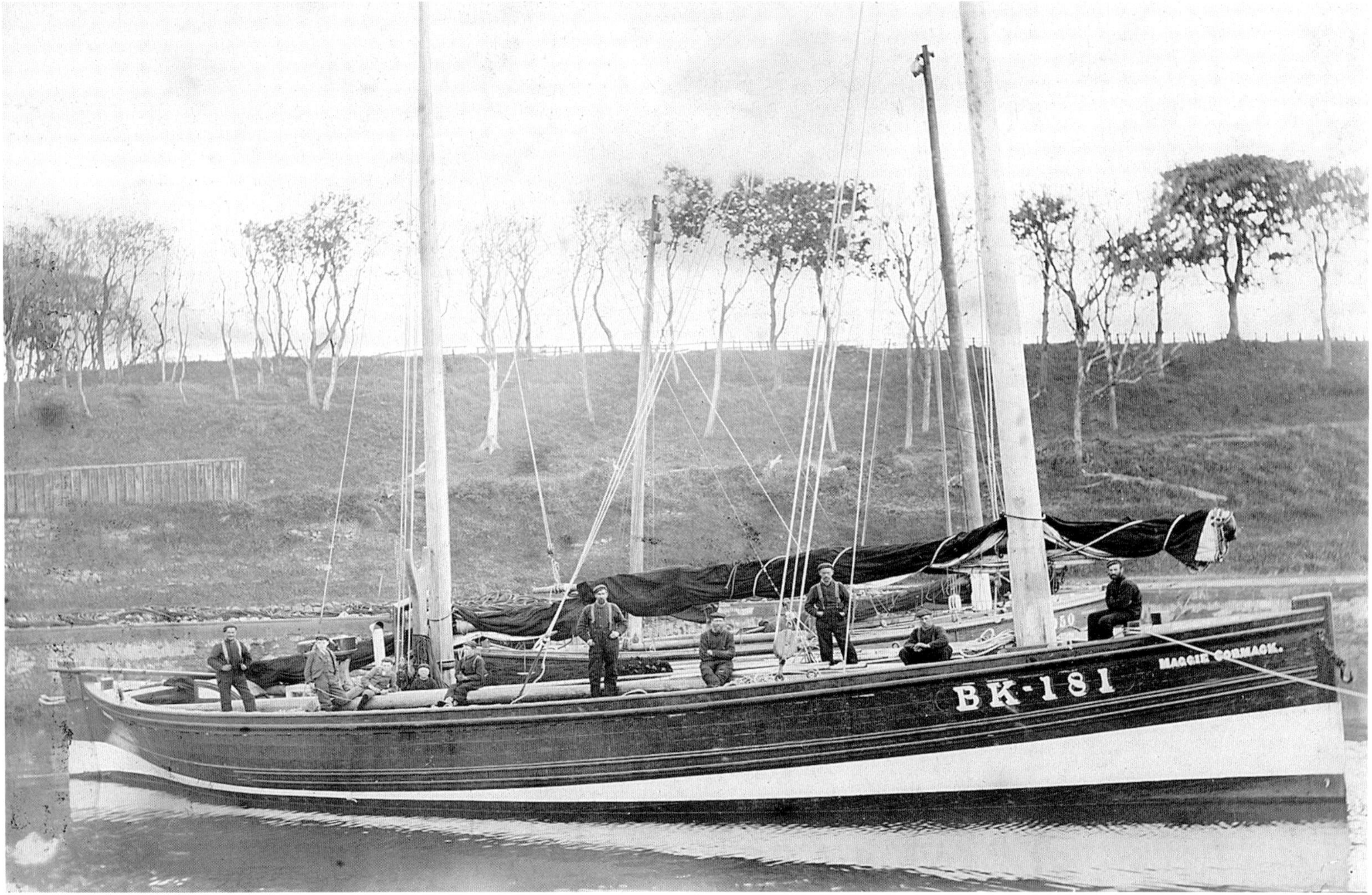

These two almost identical east coast fishing boats were built in Eyemouth by J. Weatherhead boatbuilders. BK181, the *Maggie Cormack* was the classic Fifie. The design originally from Fifeshire was one of the most popular with shipbuilders and crew alike. She was able to be recognised by her near vertical stem and stern posts. Powered by sail and oars she would have a crew of seven.

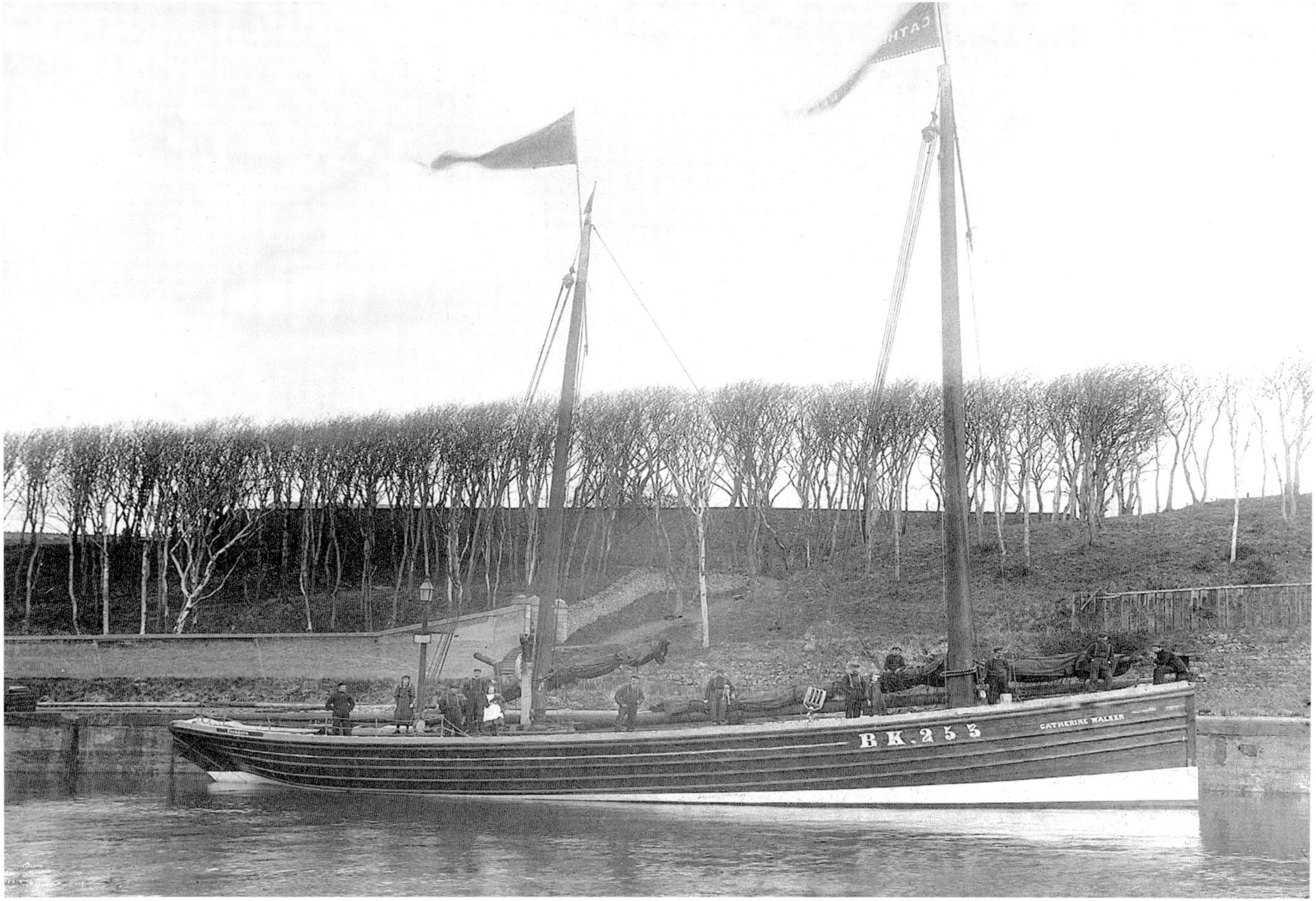

This vessel, whilst looking very similar to the *Maggie Cormack* is the BK255 *Catherine Walker* and is in fact a ship design known as a Zulu. She still had her near vertical stem post, but her stern was deeply angled. Both fishing vessels are photographed at the same time lying alongside each other opposite the entrance to Gunsgreen House. Both are pristine and newly-painted and flying their colours. They also have their family members on board, the children certainly, as the wives would never set foot on their husband's boat for fear of bad luck. The first Zulu was built in Lossiemouth in 1879, at the time of the Zulu wars, hence the name. At the end of the sail era and the introduction of petrol/paraffin engines in 1907, the men of Eyemouth were the first to realise the potential of having their boats converted. These were the *Forward; Amaranth; Dauntless* and the *Betsy Jamieson*, all large Fifies over 60 feet (18 metres) in length.

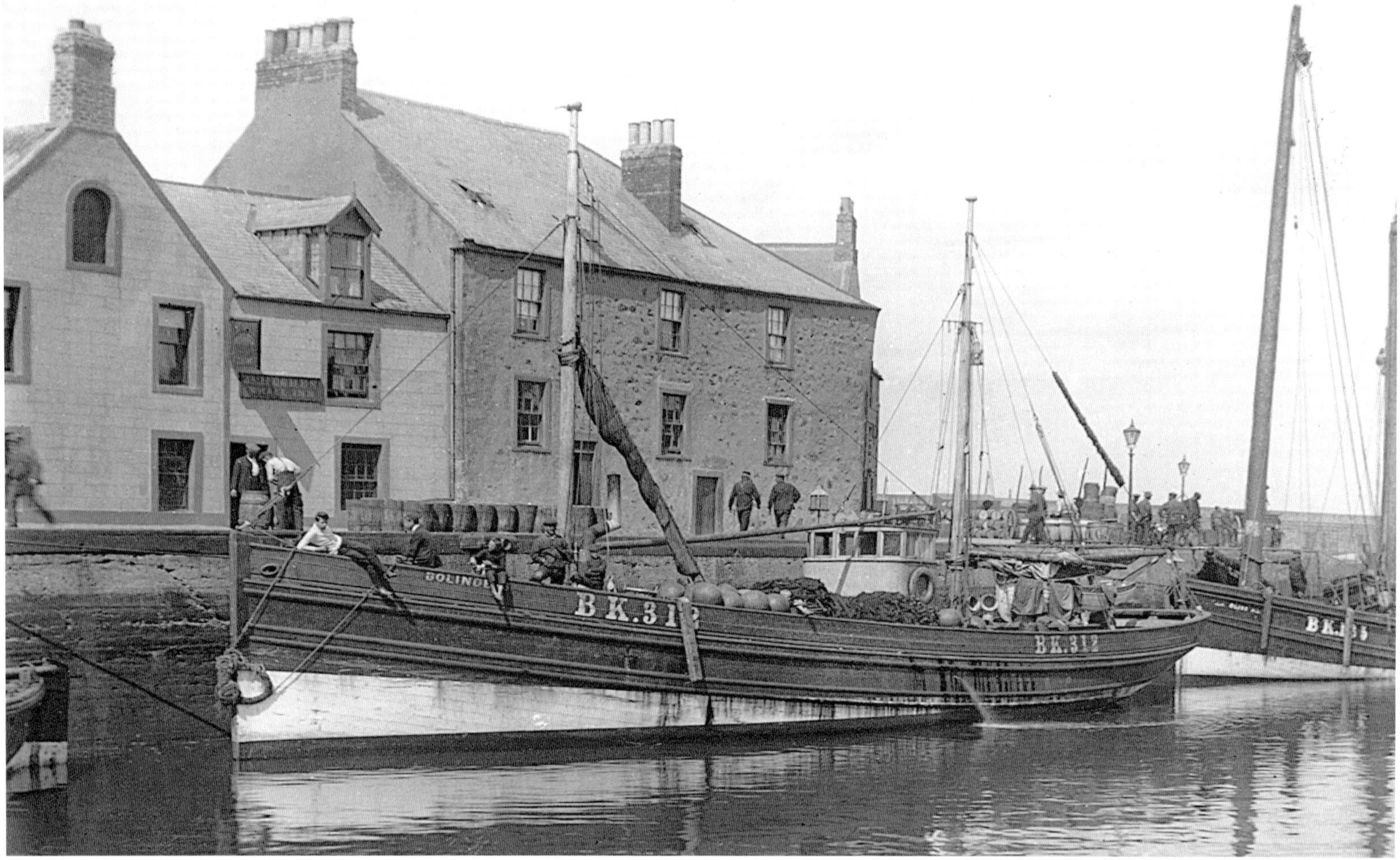

BK312, the *Bolinger*, the first Eyemouth fishing boat to convert from steam to diesel engines. Sitting opposite the old Whale Inn, the ship is laden with hemp ropes and nets and huge pigskin bladders to keep the heavy ropes afloat. The building to the right of the Whale Inn has long since been demolished and is now just an access road to a housing development further into the centre of the village. Sadly the Whale is now closed and the future of this very old pub is still uncertain. In the early 1800s there were *fourteen alehouses and one good Inn – it may be easily supposed that the effect of such a number upon the morals of the people must be most pernicious.*

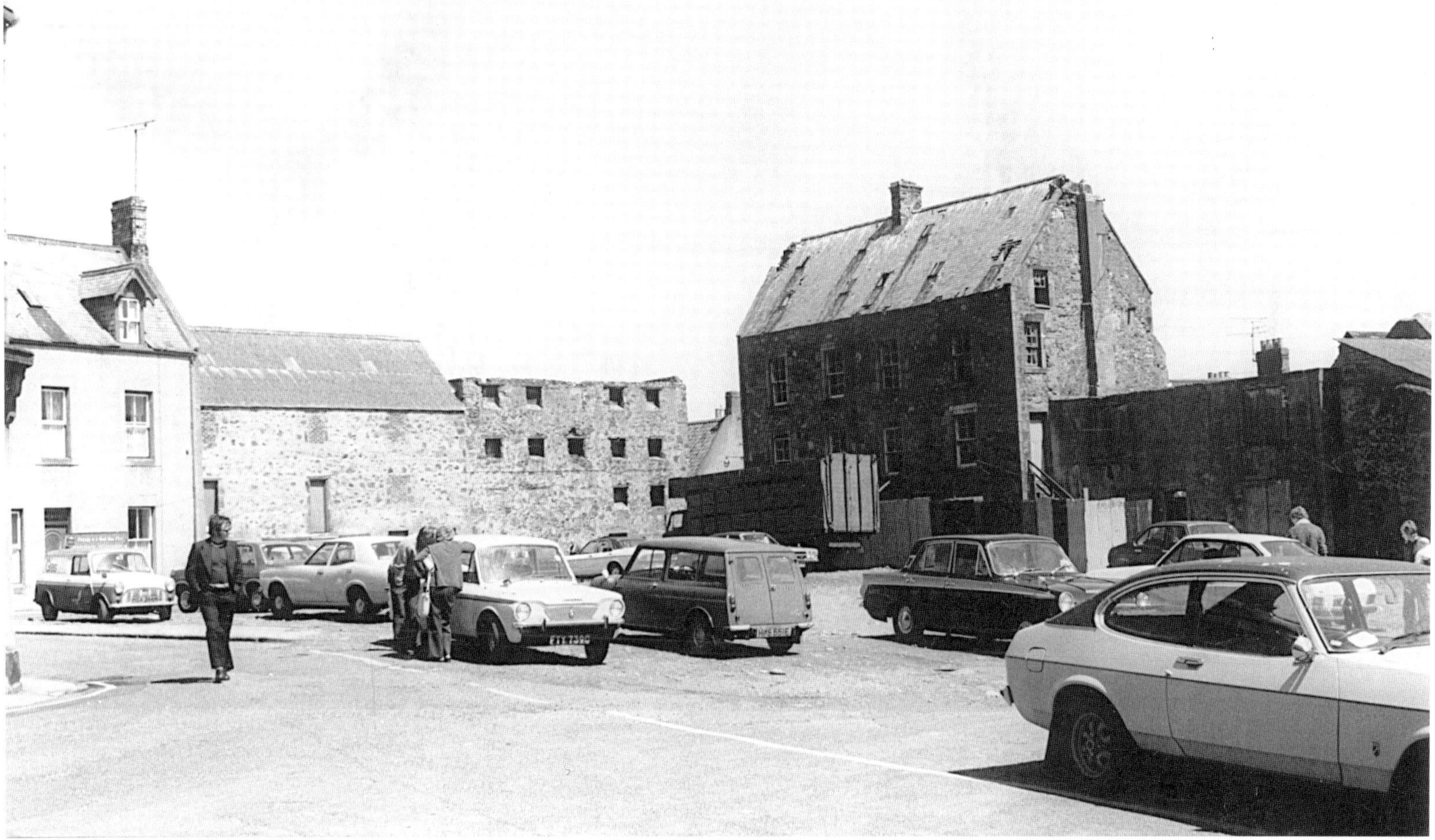

Clearly a much later photograph with the token Ford Corsair, Mini Clubman, Triumph Herald, Riley, Ford Cortina etc. This is the site now dominated by Swan Court and stretches from George Street to behind the Ship Hotel and the Fisherman's Mission. In the background we can see the last vestiges of old Eyemouth, crumbling and torn down. Glasgow Terrace still stands, but only just! Whilst Swan Court was a much-needed facility for the care of older people, the car park was sorely missed when it was phased out for development, as the town still lacks sufficient car parking.

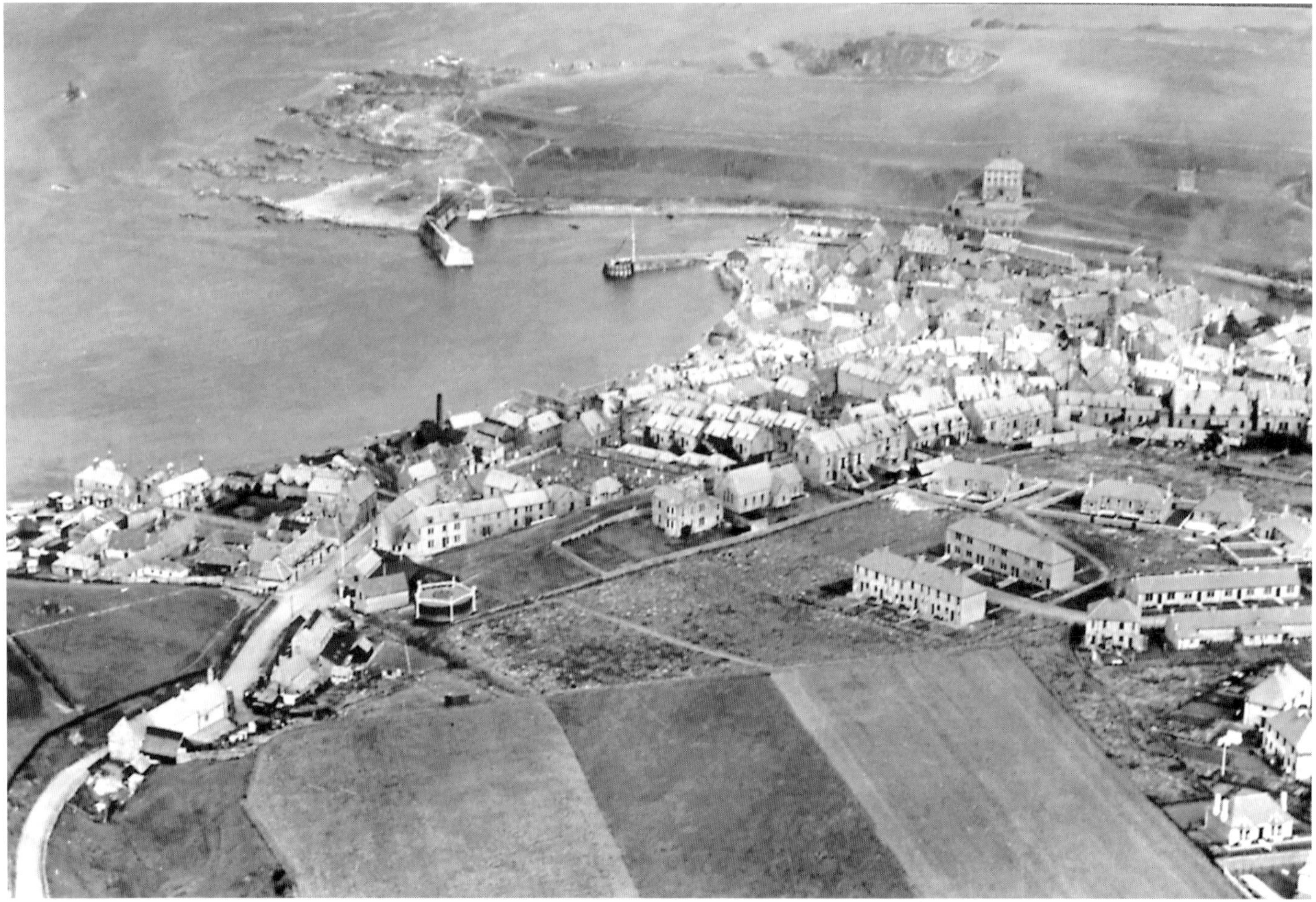

I love this juxtaposition of old Eyemouth with its tightly-packed houses amidst the narrow vennels and wynds of the town and the new housing developments of Upper Houndlaw, Seafield, St.Clair's and The Glebe. The old town shows the Hippodrome, Dixon's Yard, the Auld Kirk, Glasgow Terrace, the old gas tank and the coal gas chimney on the sea front. Northburn Farm's buildings are all standing and there looks to be a funfair in the greens just next to the farm; this area was used for the drying of fishing nets and bleaching of linens as there is a natural spring water well in the corner. The original design of Smeaton's harbour is still very evident, as is the old lifeboat shed, Gunsgreen House, of course and Cromwell's Tower, or Nisbet's Tower as it is now known.

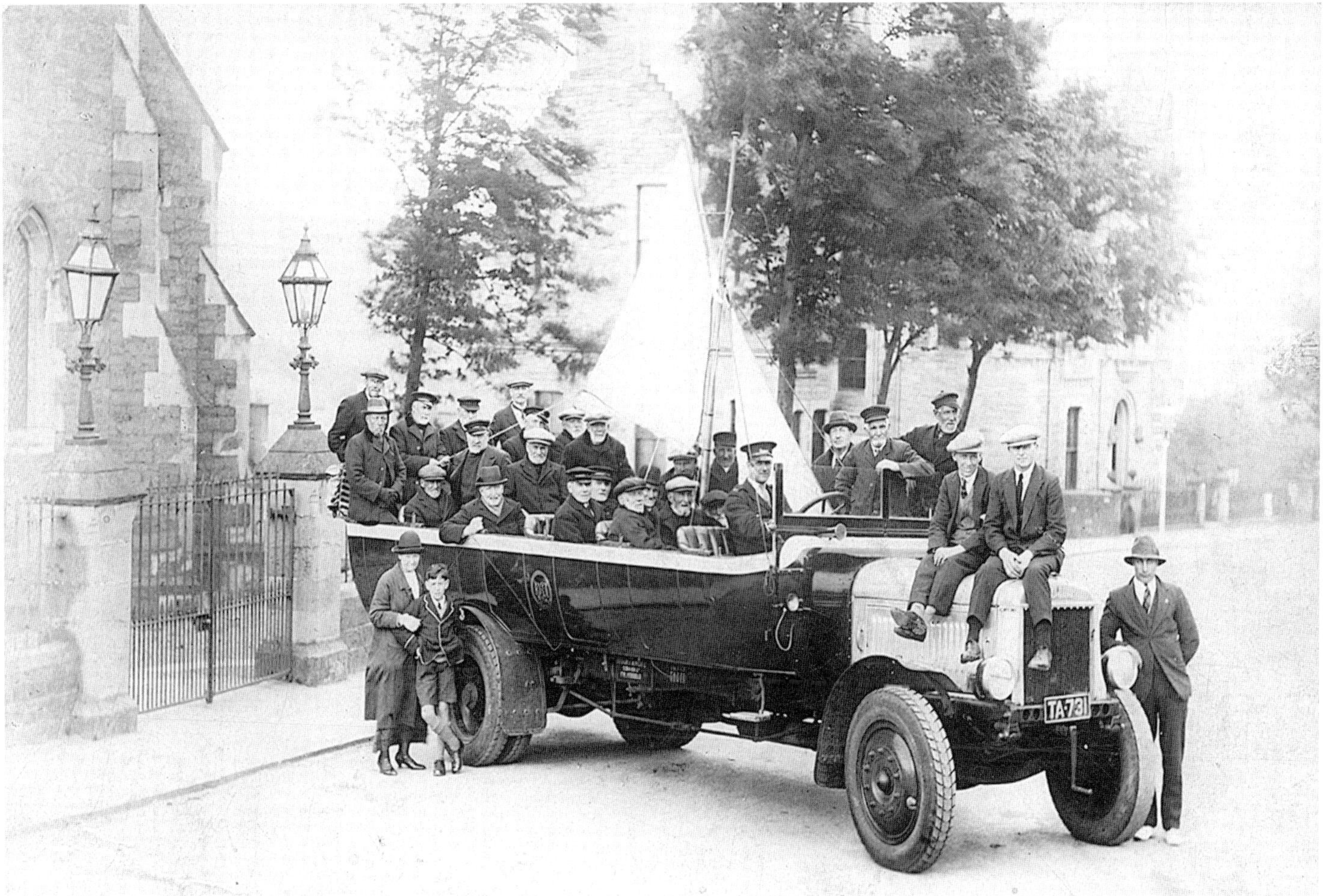

A fisherman's day out! Each year around Easter time, there would be a day trip for the skippers of the local fleet. This charabanc belonged to the Territorial Army (note the registration number) and just in case you did not realise that they were fishermen, they have erected a sail in the middle of the bus! This view is taken on the corner of the A7 road just up from the sheriff court in Selkirk. Whilst the view is not of Eyemouth, they are Eyemouth Fishermen. Incidentally, the church in the foreground has since been demolished. The fishermen also traveled to Alnwick and Leith and there is a very fine photograph available of all the lads having an ice cream!

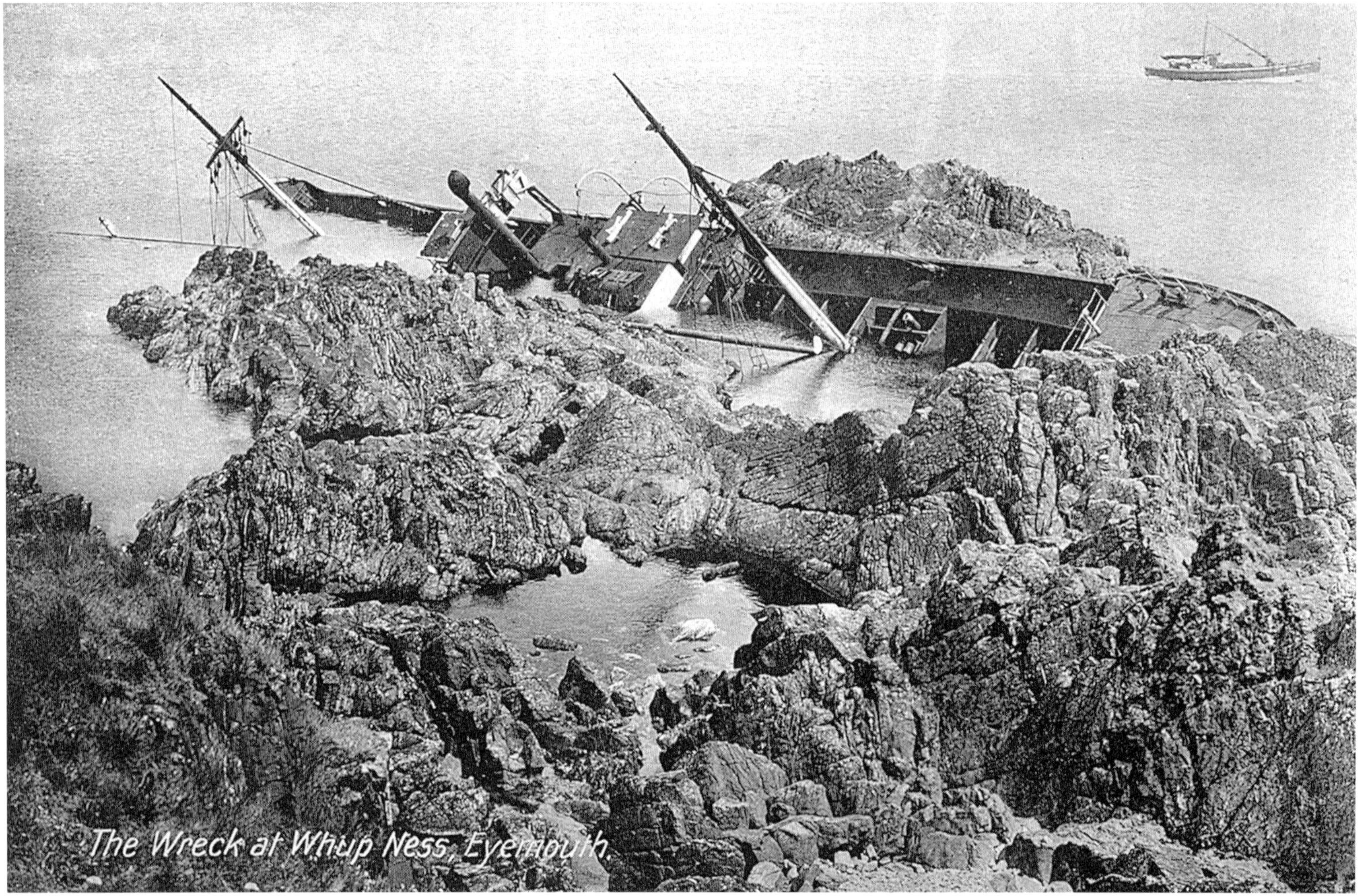

The coastal trader *President* was built and registered in Sunderland in 1907 and was travelling from Hamburg, Germany to Methil in Fife when she ran aground in thick fog on 29th April 1928. The rocky reef which she struck is known as Whup Ness. Weighing 1,946 gross tons she quickly became wedged in the rocks. Fortunately all of the crew managed to scramble ashore and the lifeboat was not called out. The weather deteriorated and the ship quickly broke into pieces. Being so close to Eyemouth Harbour, the site is now a very popular scuba dive, as there are still interesting artefacts to be seen.

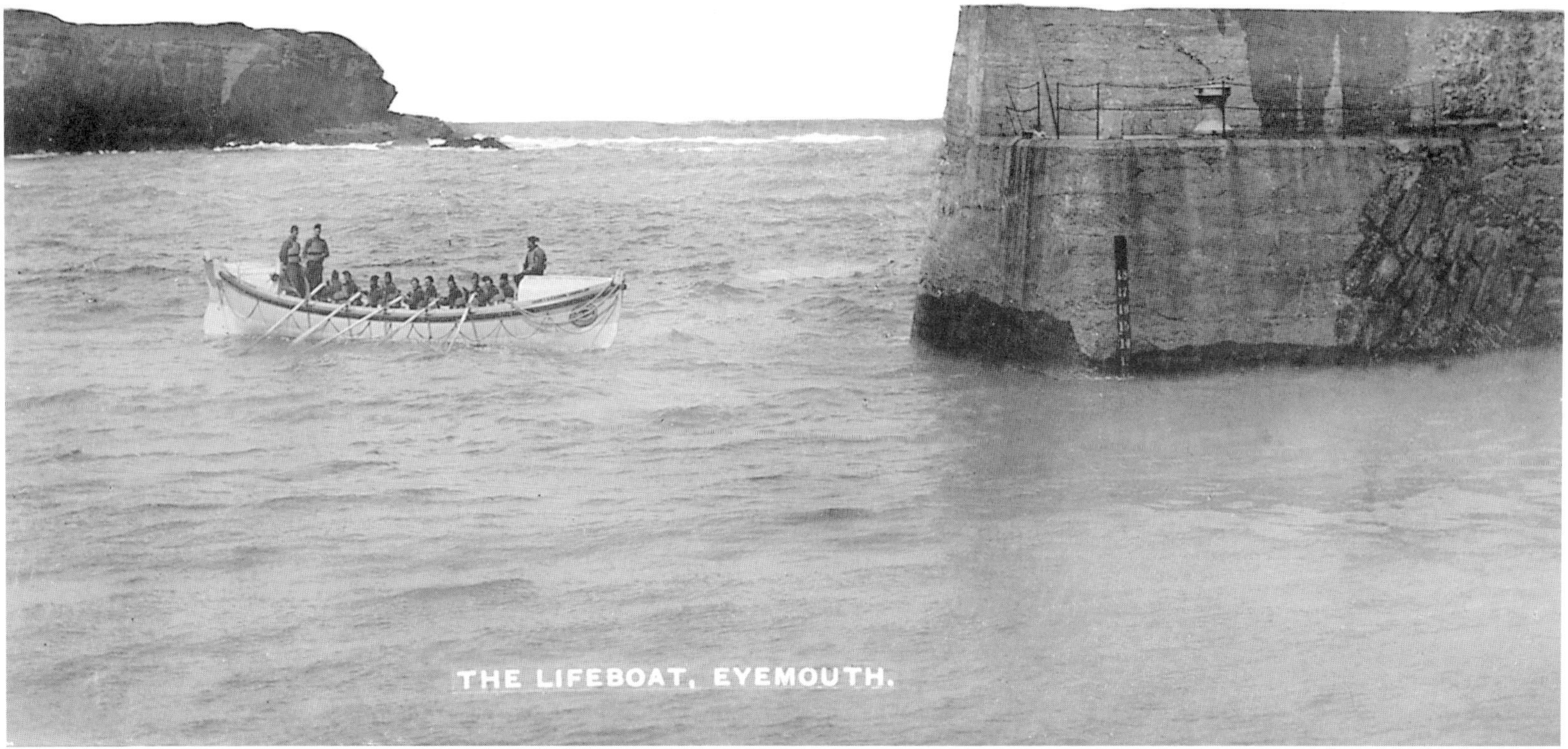

How the radical designs of the lifeboat have changed since their inception. This is the *James and Rachel Grindley* seen here at the harbour entrance. On her first ever rescue mission, her crew escorted 21 fishing boats from outside the 'Roadsteads' to the safety of the inner harbour, assisting in the rescue of 120 men, by means of rowing outside the safety of the bay 21 times to bring each boat to safety in the storm!

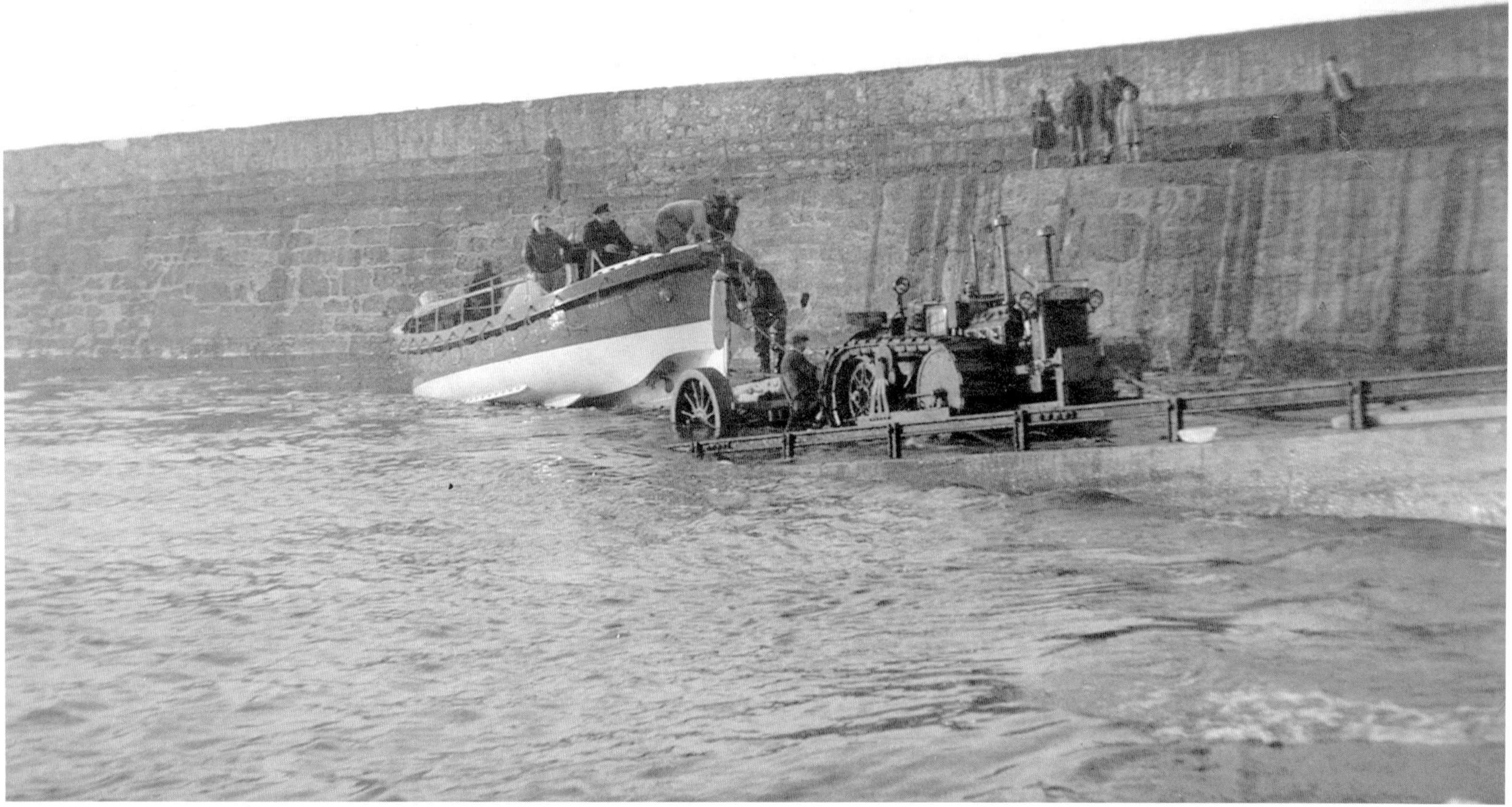

As the design changed and improvements were made to the lifeboat, a new lifeboat shed was also built to house the craft. The lifeboat needed a special caterpillar-tracked tractor to haul her back out of the water after a successful launch and mission. The old pierhead, originally built by Smeaton, faced into Eyemouth Bay, but the lifeboat could only be launched at part full tide, as there was always too much sand collected at the harbour entrance on the 'Bar'. It would be many years before a new harbour entrance would be built. Now the latest in technological lifeboats is stationed in Eyemouth and is capable of reaching far distances in virtually any weather conditions.

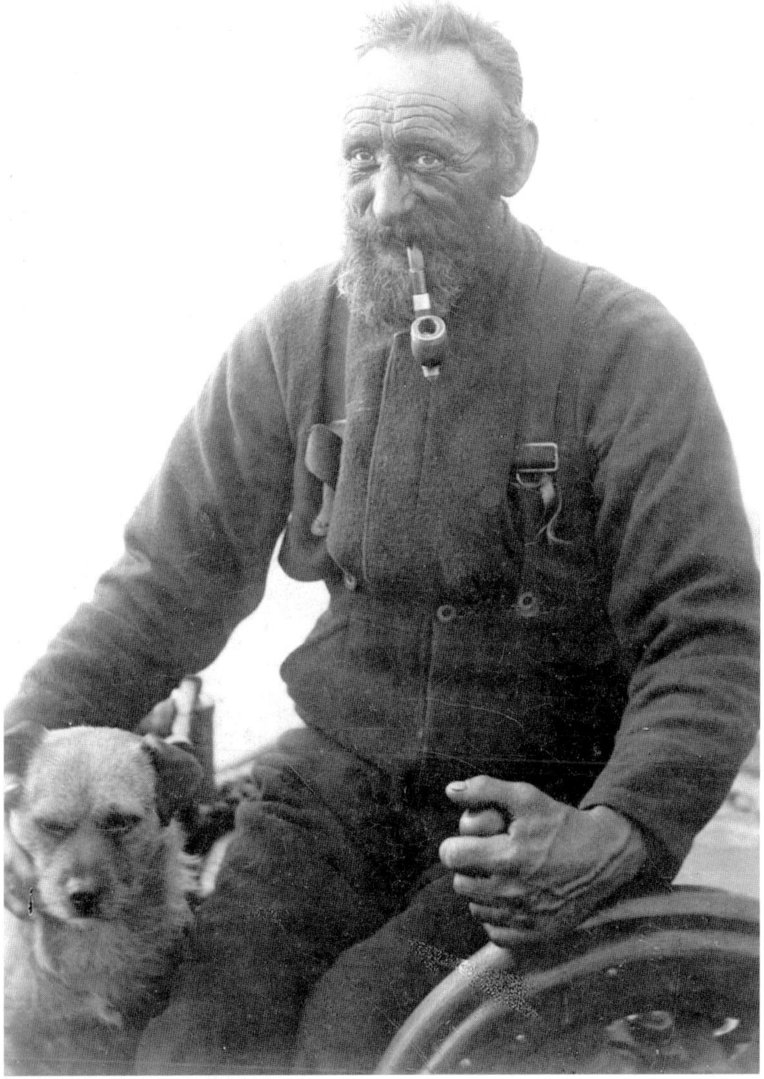

If ever a picture tells the story of the sea and the fishermen of Eyemouth, then it is this. The deeply-lined face and faraway look to the eyes are one aspect, the deeply-veined and very strong hand at the steering wheel are a powerful symbol, yet the other hand around his friend tell of a kindness underneath the strong exterior.

Burnmouth is now actually five villages. Flemington or Upper Burnmouth was first founded back in the twelfth century and is in the parish of Ayton. The village inevitably blossomed around the railway terminus and 'Doon the Brae' consists of Lower Burnmouth, Partanhall, Ross and Cowdrait. It was described back in 1913 as being entered around a huge boulder which lay at one end of Lower Burnmouth with the other end terminating in a cliff. Partanhall is the most northerly of the three villages and has changed little over the last couple of centuries. The huge boulder is long gone, to aid vehicular traffic and Lower Burnmouth, in the centre and closest to the harbour has changed with the addition of a few houses to the northern side with net stores built underneath the houses. Ross, furthest to the south now consists of only four houses and adjoins Cowdrait (at the southern edge of the coast) which has changed the most with virtually all of the original 'clat and clay' cottages knocked down and built up as council houses. Most of these have since been sold and whilst there is still a local population at this end of the village, like small coastal villages all along the east coast, the majority are holiday homes.

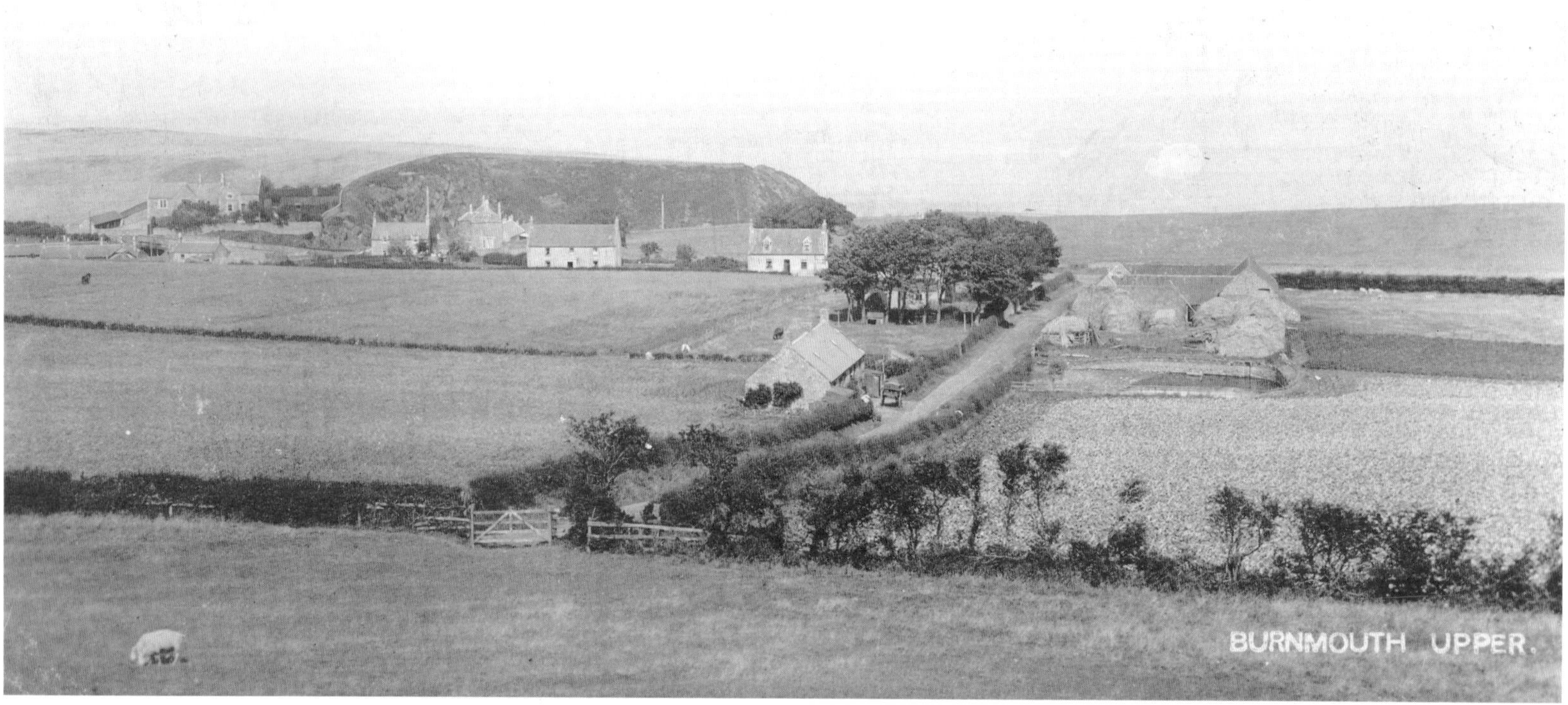

Upper Burnmouth, originally known as Flemington, after the Flemish who settled in the area. The old farm in the foreground is known as East Flemington and the building in the centre of the photograph is the former Flemington Inn, which burned to the ground a few years ago. The view is taken from the Chesters, the large rise behind Burnmouth where Chesterbank Farm is located. Chester, of course, is the old Roman name for fort and there have been several ancient finds up on this strategic hill. The view has considerably changed with a new row of cottages leading up from the farm road. The trees are gone, the Flemington Inn is gone, but there are many new homes.

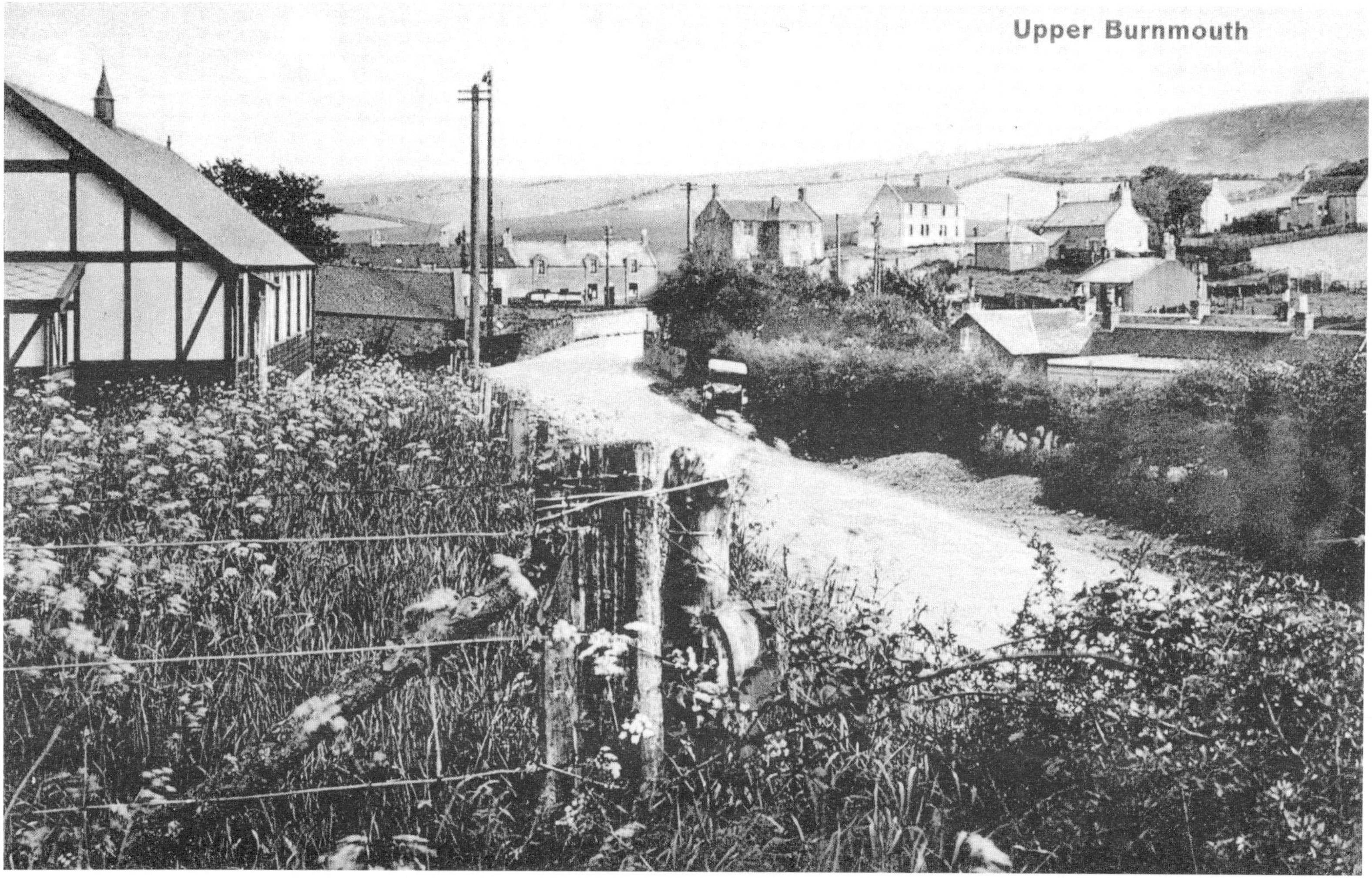

The old road leading from Eyemouth ran in past the old hall and the school where you could either turn down the Gorge to Lower Burnmouth, or continue sharp right and over the railway bridge to get to Burnmouth Station and thence onwards to the main road to Berwick and the south, or northwards through Ayton to Edinburgh. Whilst the view has little changed, other than more houses, this was the main road linking Eyemouth to the A1 before a new connection was made at Redhall in Eyemouth.

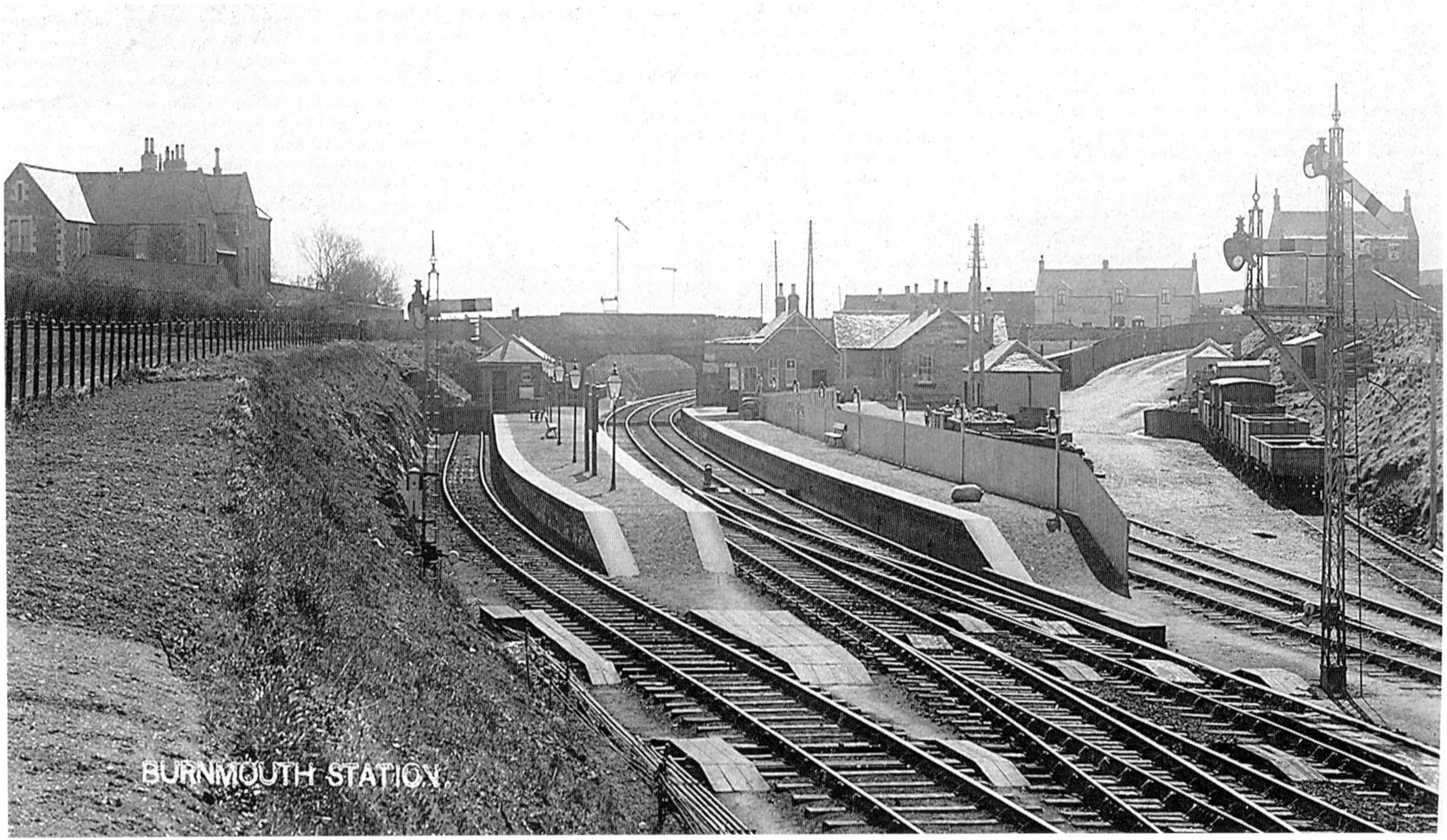

A very early photograph of the Burnmouth Station terminus, showing all of the interleaved railway lines. This terminus first opened in 1846 and served the local community and fishing industry until 1962. The siding to the extreme right ran up the brae towards the main road between Eyemouth and Burnmouth. This small branch was installed to service Burnmouth Harbour which had its own fleet of fishing boats. The daily catch was loaded onto horse and cart and carried up the brae to be further re-loaded onto the goods wagons at the railway station. The branch to the extreme left handled the branch line from Eyemouth, with a link to the main line where the goods wagons filled with fish were transferred. For such a small village, the introduction of the railway station expanded the town of Upper Burnmouth and a new school was built. Now all five, separate, yet interconnected hamlets are known collectively as Burnmouth.

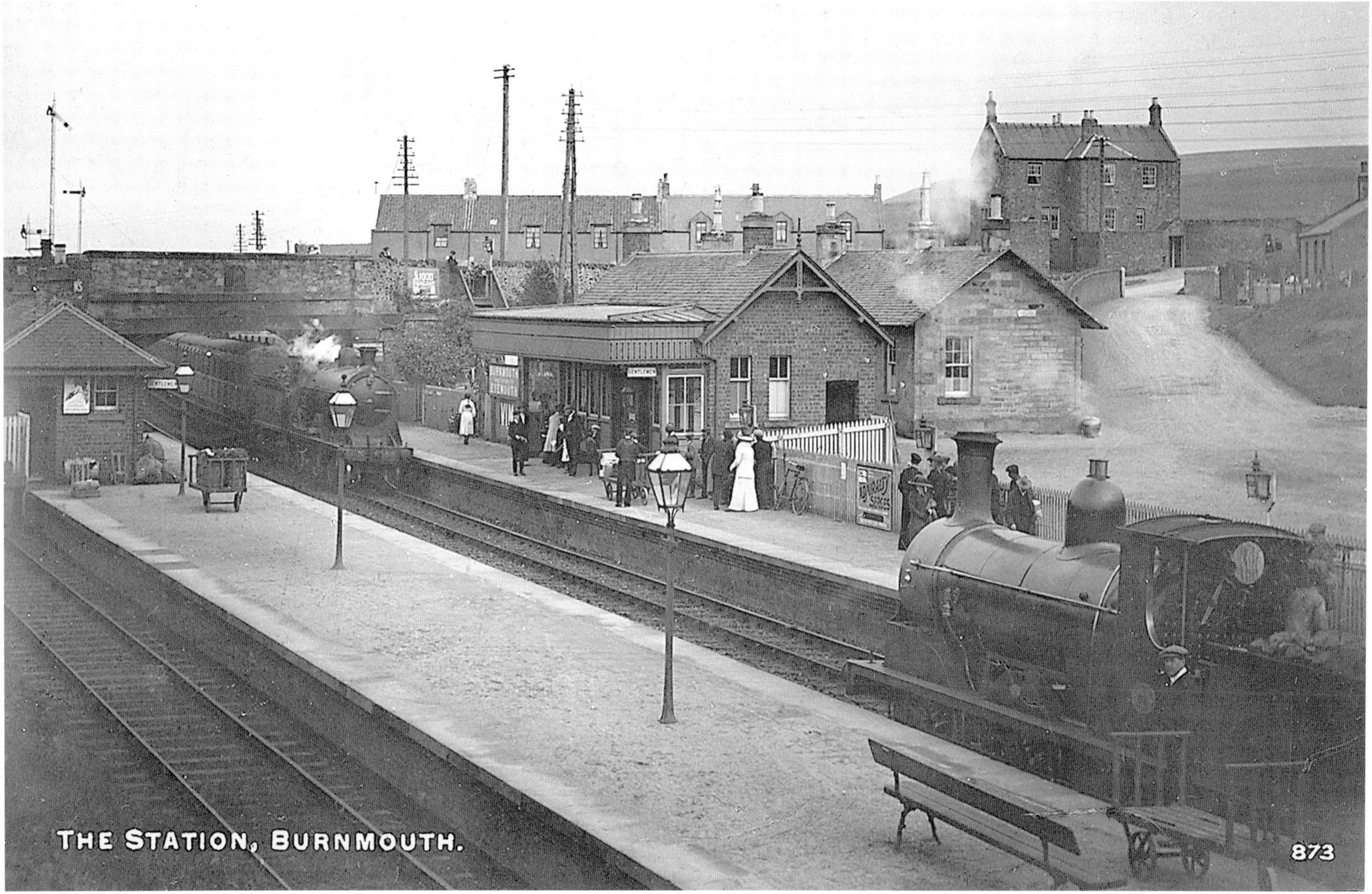

Whilst the previous photograph of Burnmouth Railway Station showed the siding to the right, this even earlier photograph shows the road with no sidings constructed. The siding was built was to facilitate the rising freight from the local harbour. It would be a fair assumption to reason that these passengers would be crossing the bridge and to the other side of the railway track to catch the 'Eight Minute Link' to Eyemouth.

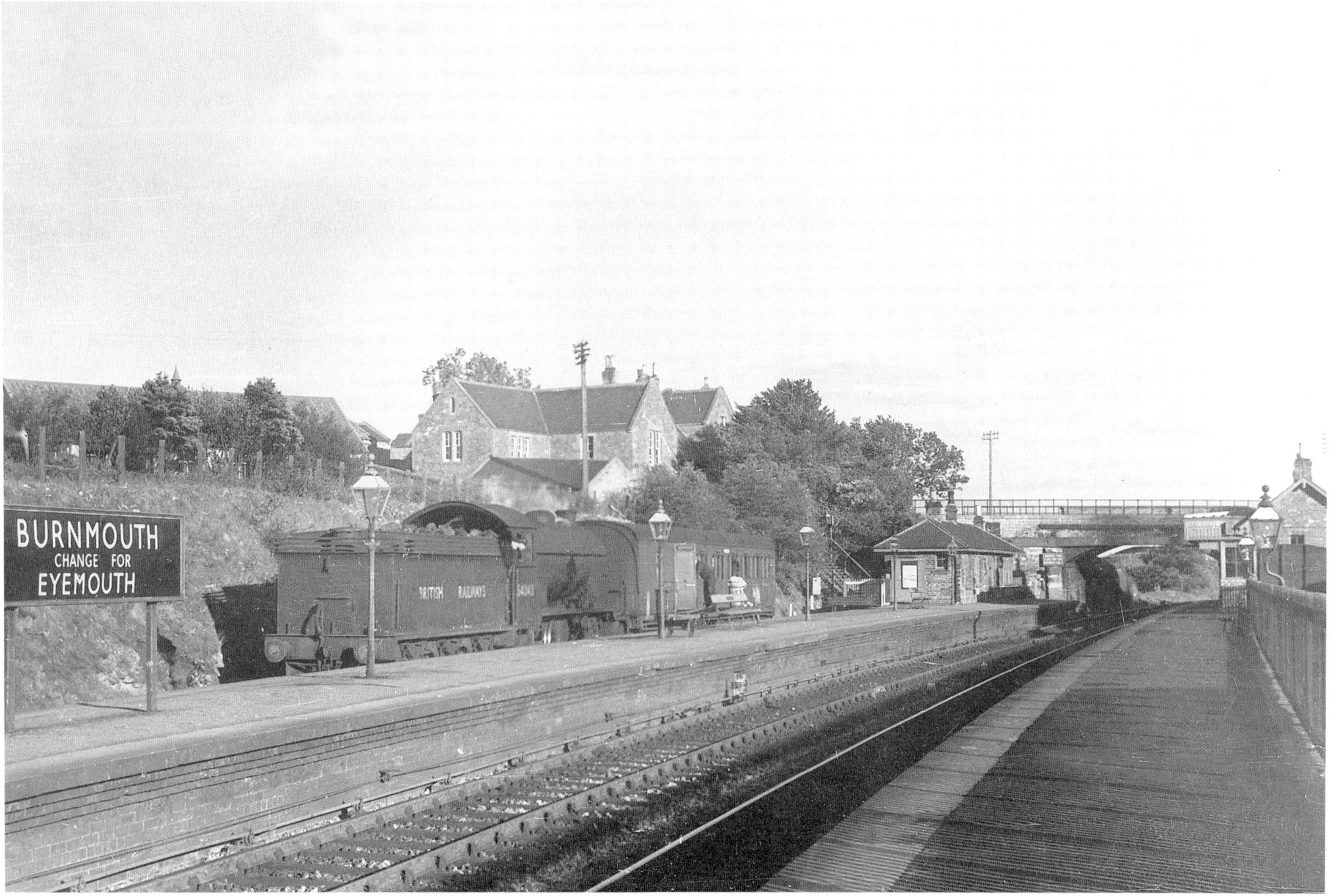

Burnmouth Station now installed with the branch line for Eyemouth which was opened on April 13th 1891. Used predominantly for freight carriage of fish from the quayside, it soon became evident that tourists also enjoyed this incredibly scenic trip to Eyemouth.

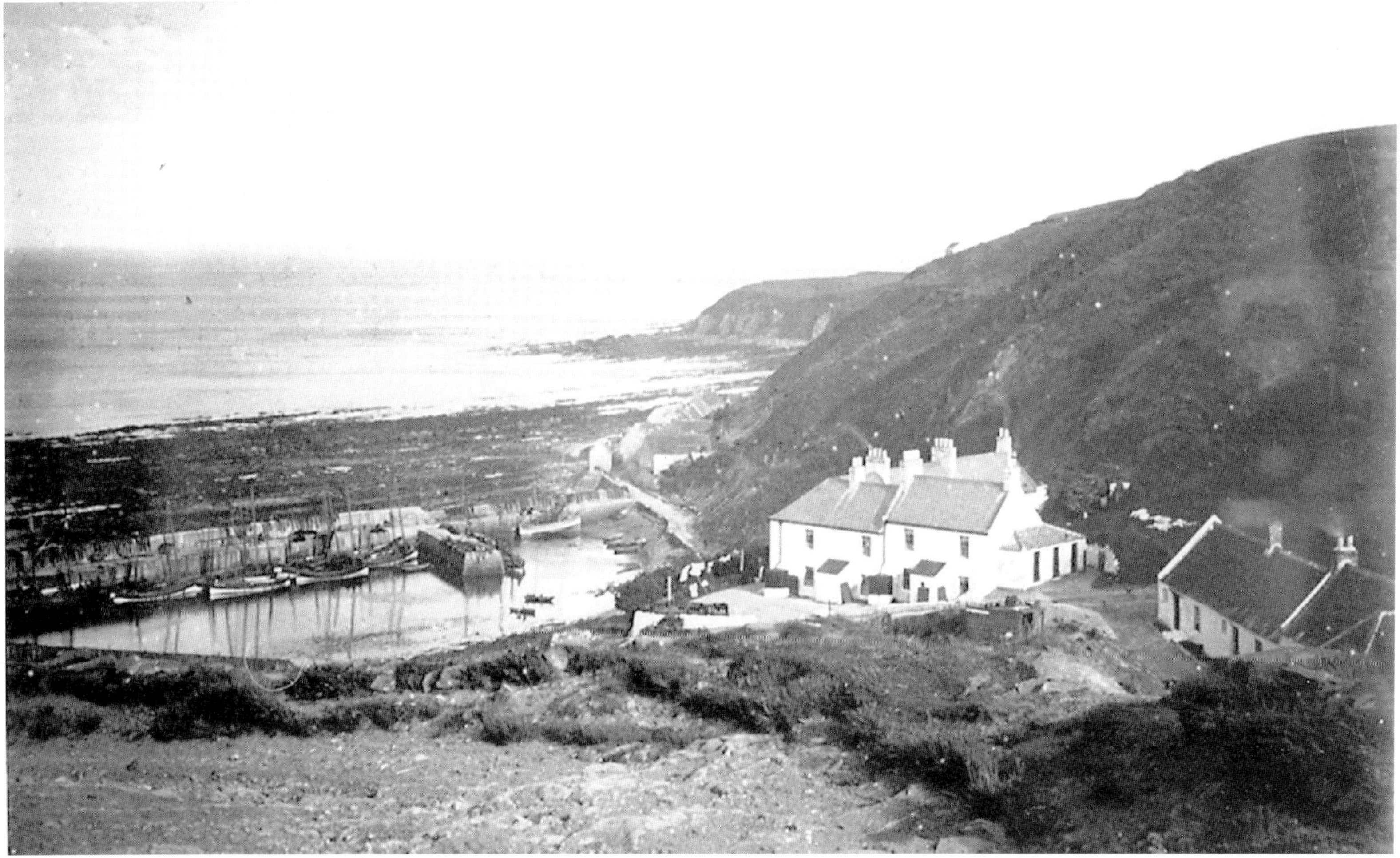

Whilst it is unclear when this photograph was taken, we do know that it is was before work was started to convert the old Mission Hall, in fact it was taken before the Mission Hall was even built in 1888, as the people of Burnmouth raised sufficient funds to take over the feu for the hall and have it converted into a church in 1897. The new United Presbyterian Church was officially opened in 1898 with Alexander Urquart inducted as its first minister. Looking at the harbour in the background and the sailing ships in the harbour, this photograph also predates 1879 when the second extension to the harbour was built, forming an inner harbour.

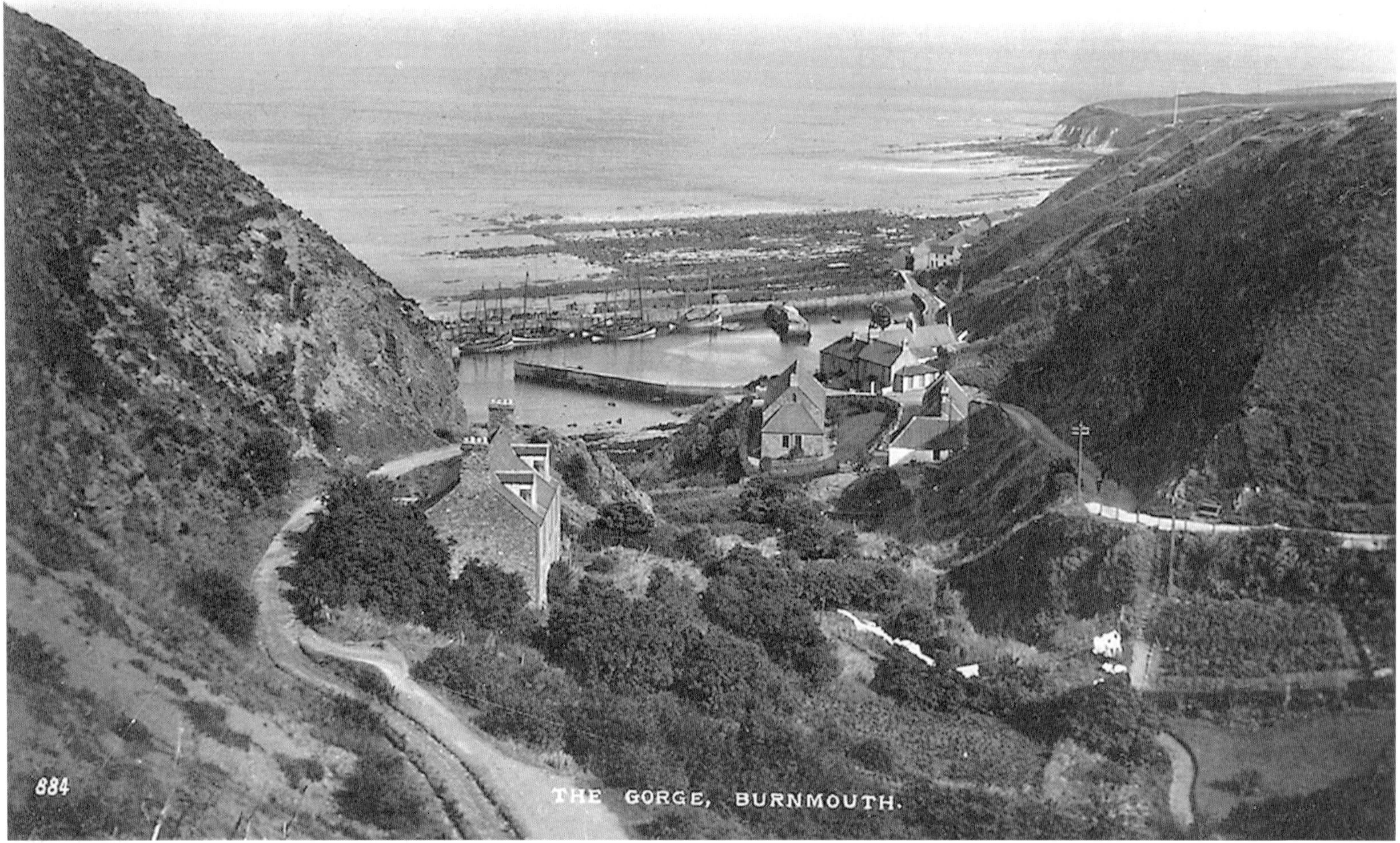

A view down the Gorge, but now the church has been built. In the picture the row of cottages to the right of the church are still intact, but it would not be long before they were knocked down and the road widened on that corner to aid traffic up and down the Brae. The harbour works are completed, but the vessels are still sailing ships. The track skirting the northern limit of the gorge to the left of the picture is the back road to Partanhall.

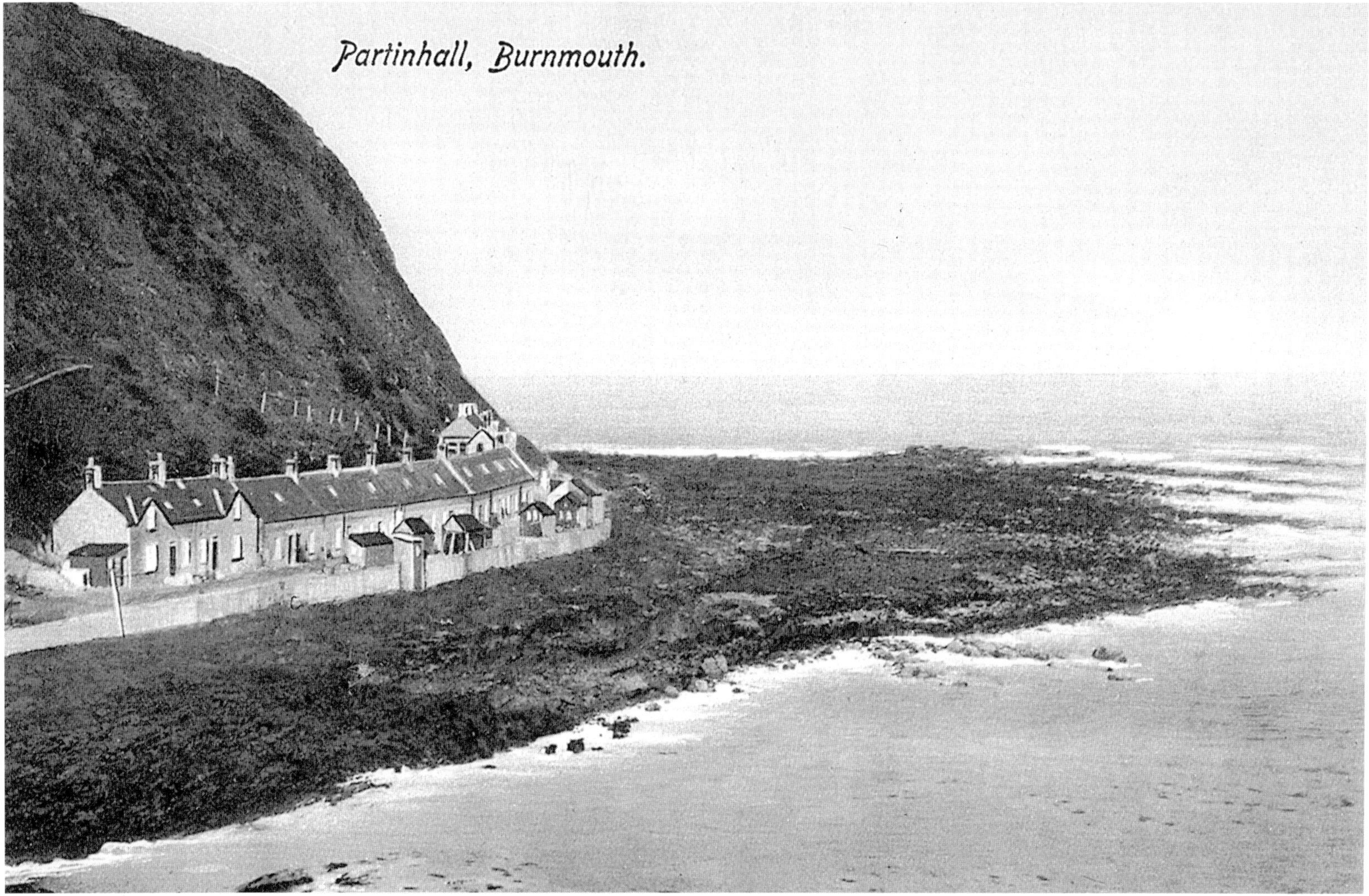

A slight spelling mistake, but in fact virtually all villages change spelling as the dialect and inflection of words also changes. This hamlet is virtually unchanged nestled at the foot of the Gorge. Between Partanhall and the harbour were several old upturned boats which had been converted into crofts and storage sheds and at least three families lived in these recycled boats at one time.

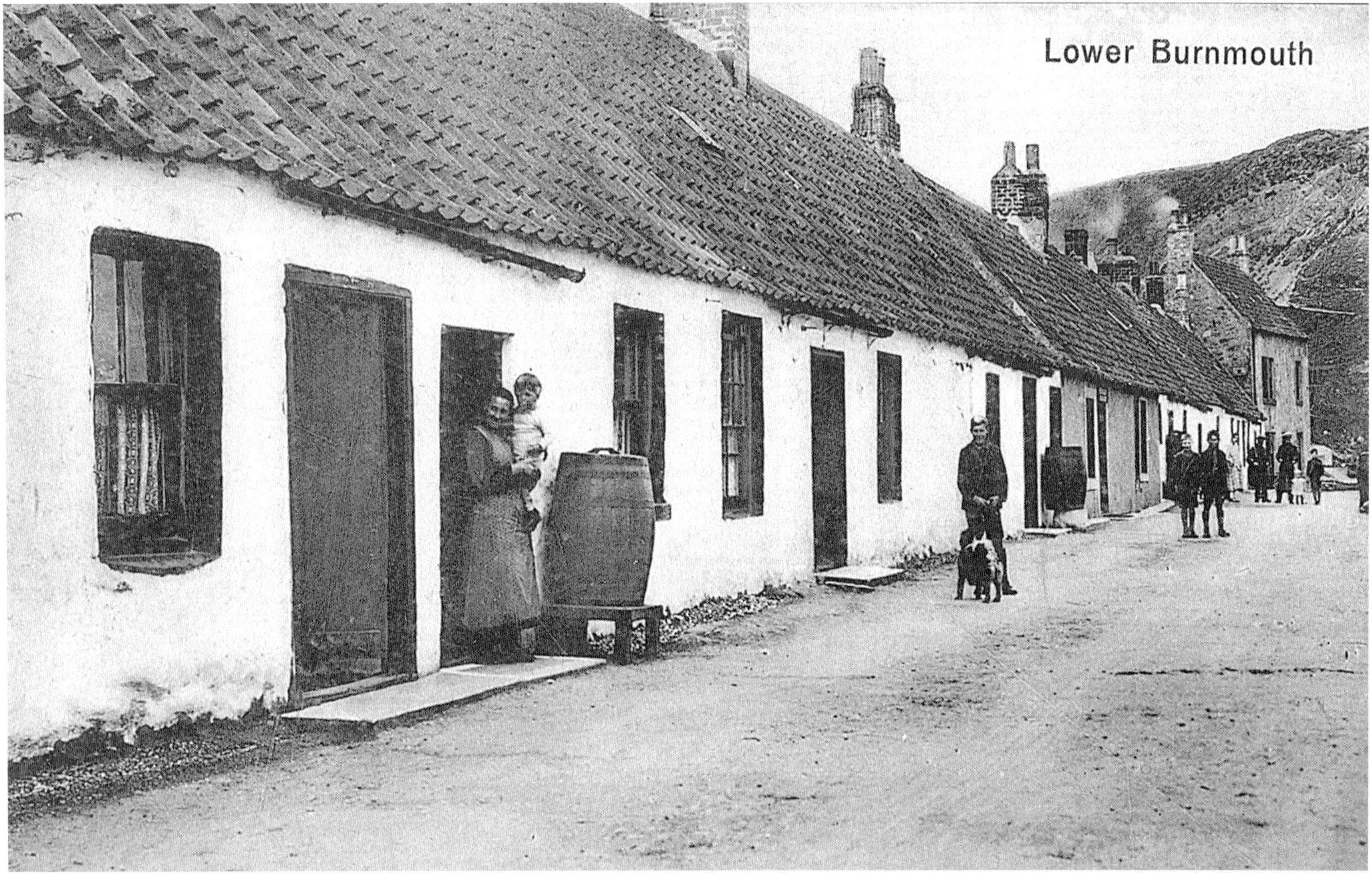

Lower Burnmouth was located directly next to the harbour and comprised of around fourteen cottages and three smoke houses for the herring. With no running water, rain water was collected from roof run-off and also from the Burn itself which still flows down the Gorge and terminates near the old coastguard apparatus shed. Virtually all of these buildings have been demolished and Lower Burnmouth is closer to the harbourside now with more modern buildings built in the late 1950s by Berwickshire District Council.

Photographed in Cowdrait with a view of the cliffs above Partanhall in the background, the fisherman is preparing a pitch solution with horse hair to apply onto the seams of his boat to make them watertight. His work shed is a former boat turned upside down which has seen better days. The local crab and lobster pots or craves are lying to the side and another couple of fishermen look on at the photographer as chickens run around their feet.

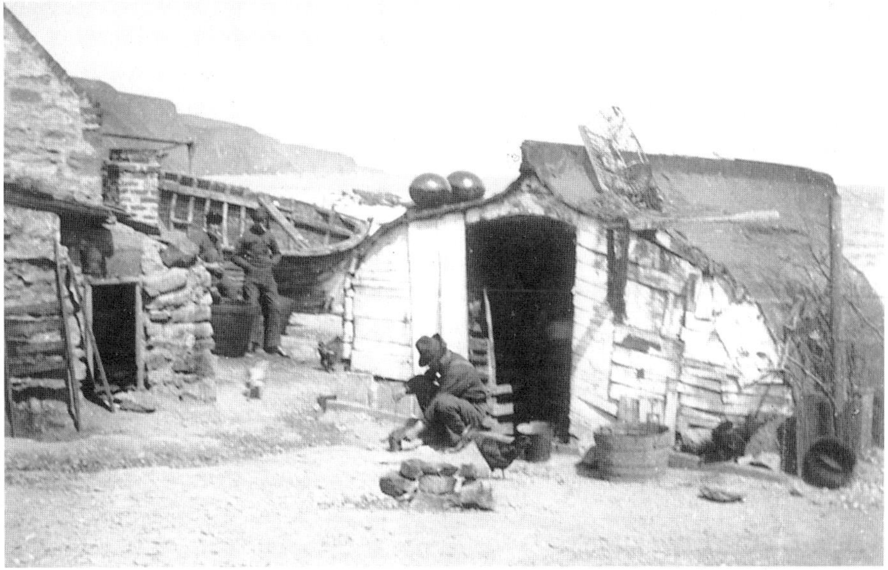

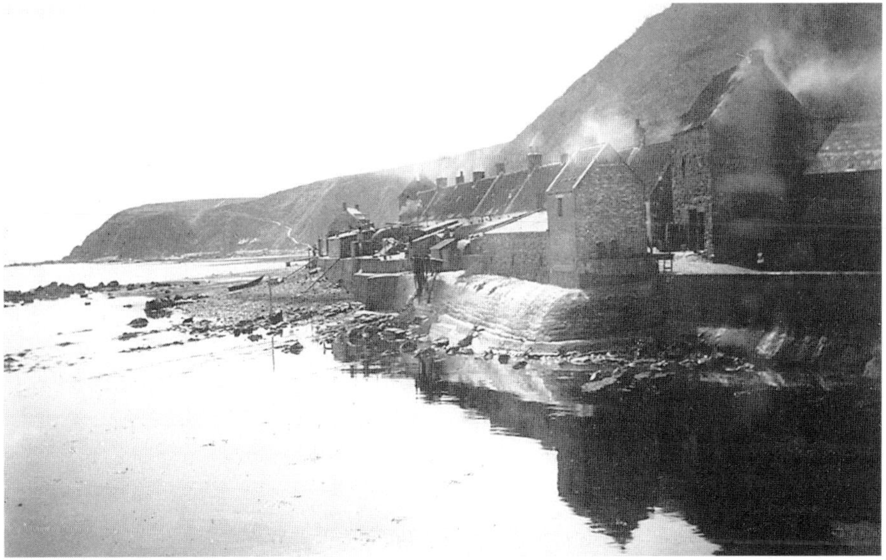

A rather smoky scene, photographed from the harbour wall. During the herring season, fishing boats from all over the British Isles would descend on the little coastal village, following the migrating herring. Not only are there smoking lums from the houses, there were also three smoke houses in operation in Lower Burnmouth. I imagine that the village must have stank during the season.

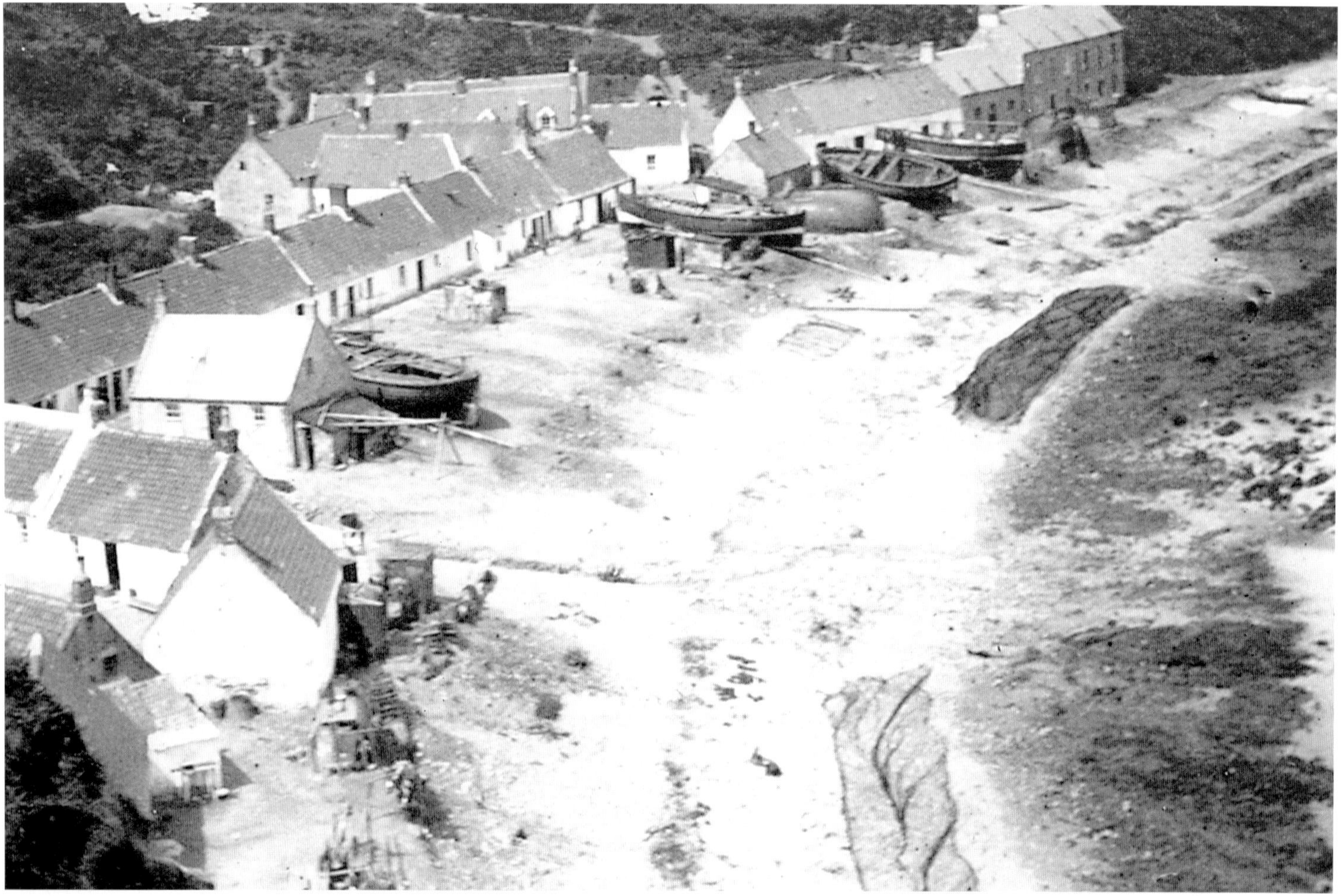

Cowdrait, with the village of Ross in the lower corner was an archetypal fishing community, so common along the coast of Scotland. The old 'clat and clay' houses are perched precariously close to the waters' edge and the small summer boats or lobster and crab boats are pulled up onto the foreshore. This section of Burnmouth has peculiar ridges of rock strata which run parallel to the shore, thereby reducing the energy from the large sea waves on the high tide. This geological formation allowed the houses to be built close to the water's edge. Hemp nets can be seen drying on the foreshore and further up the side of the hill, we can see someone's washing bleaching in the sun.

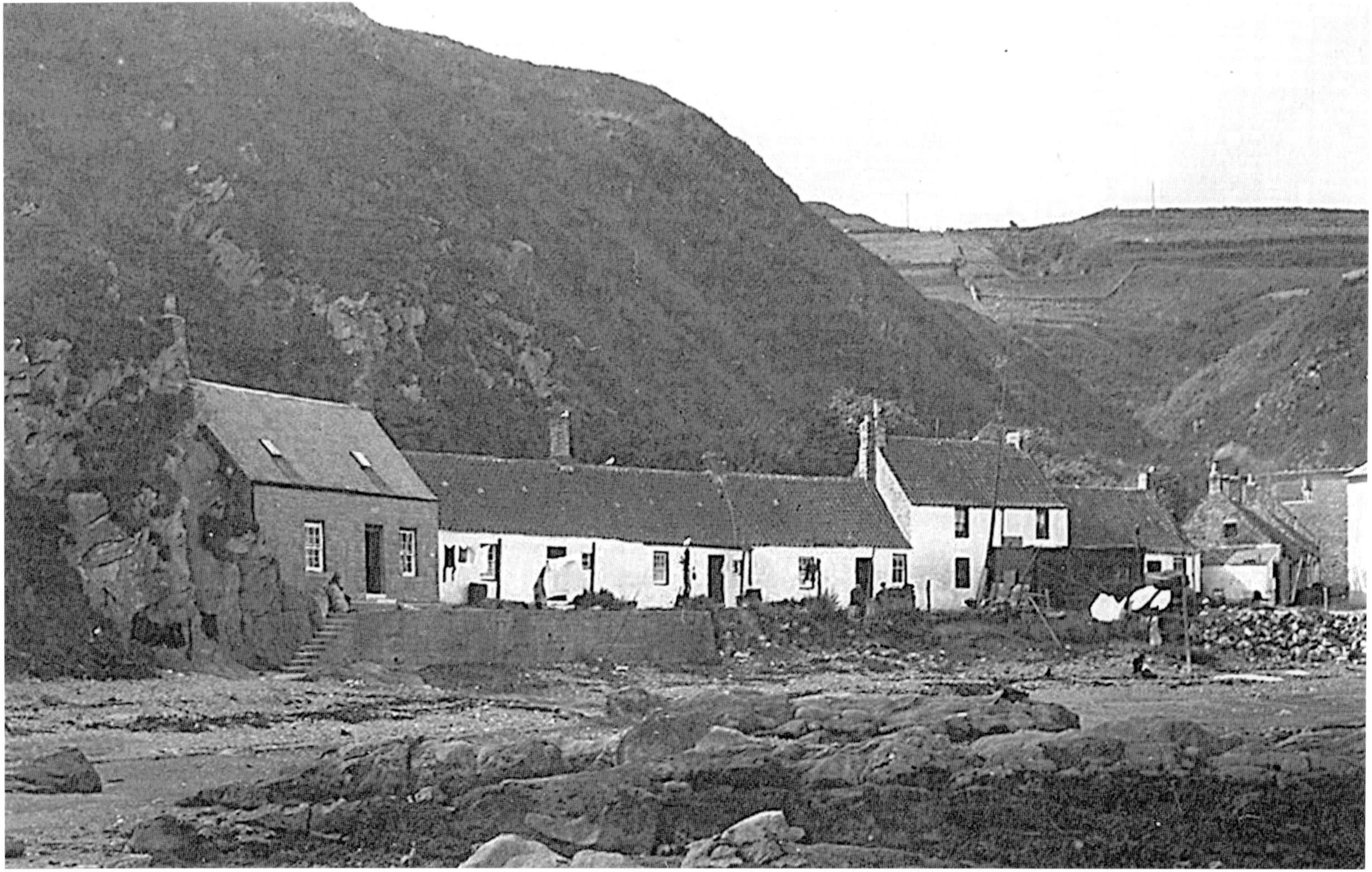

The original village of Ross, located in the Parish of Mordington and situated furthest south along the coast when coming Doon the Brae. The last house has featured in many different postcards with the owner seen mending nets etc. Looking in the distance behind the houses, there was a second burn that run down to the sea. It was this constant source of fresh water which inevitably dictated the location of all coastal villages as the only fresh water came from streams, burns and rain water collection.

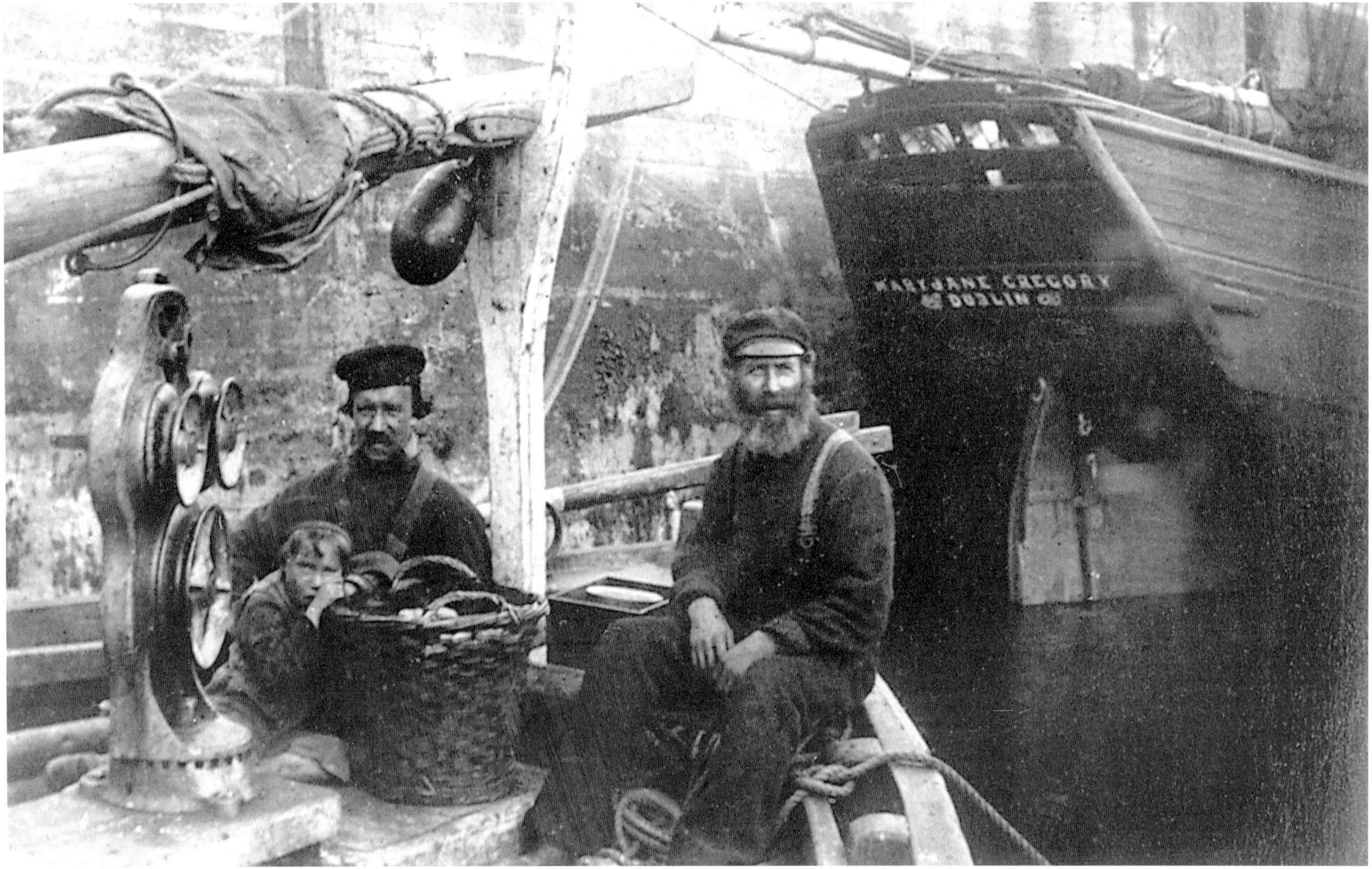

The *Mary Jane Gregory* from Dublin was one of the larger schooners which visited Burnmouth delivering empty herring barrels and collecting a fresh cargo of salted herrings or smoked 'red herrings' for the European market, principally Russia and Germany before the Great War heralded the collapse of this export trade. The two fishermen with the young boy on the fishing boat in front of the schooner are wearing a variety of headgear which denotes their position as members of the crew.

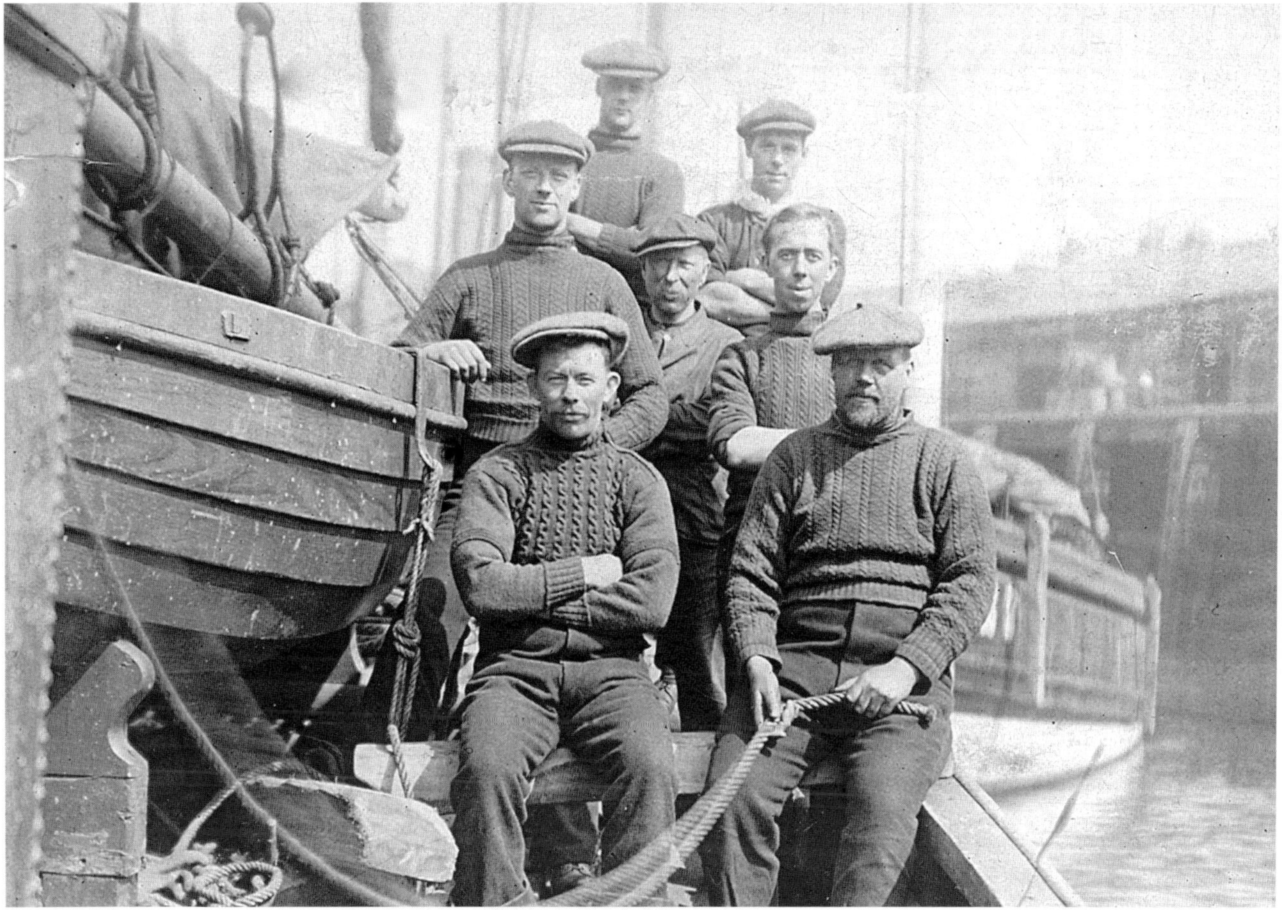

As you can see from these likely lads, they are in their Sunday best. Rather, they are each kitted out in their own distinctive *Ganseys* (or Guernsey). These fishermen's jumpers have been made on the island of Guernsey since the sixteenth Century and it was known that Mary Queen of Scots owned a Guernsey. Nelson recommended them to the Admiralty as a valuable article of naval clothing. Very few inshore fishermen could swim and it was thought unnecessary to be able to, as the water was so cold. Also once the men donned their big oilskin jackets and heavy sea boots, anyone being washed over the side would surely perish just from the weight of their garments alone. This is a rather long-winded way of telling the story of these Guernseys, as each family member was knitted a distinctive design by his wife with four needles and no stitching anywhere. Should the fisherman be lost overboard and drowned, the Guernsey was so strongly made that it would keep the body intact and identifiable solely through the pattern used.

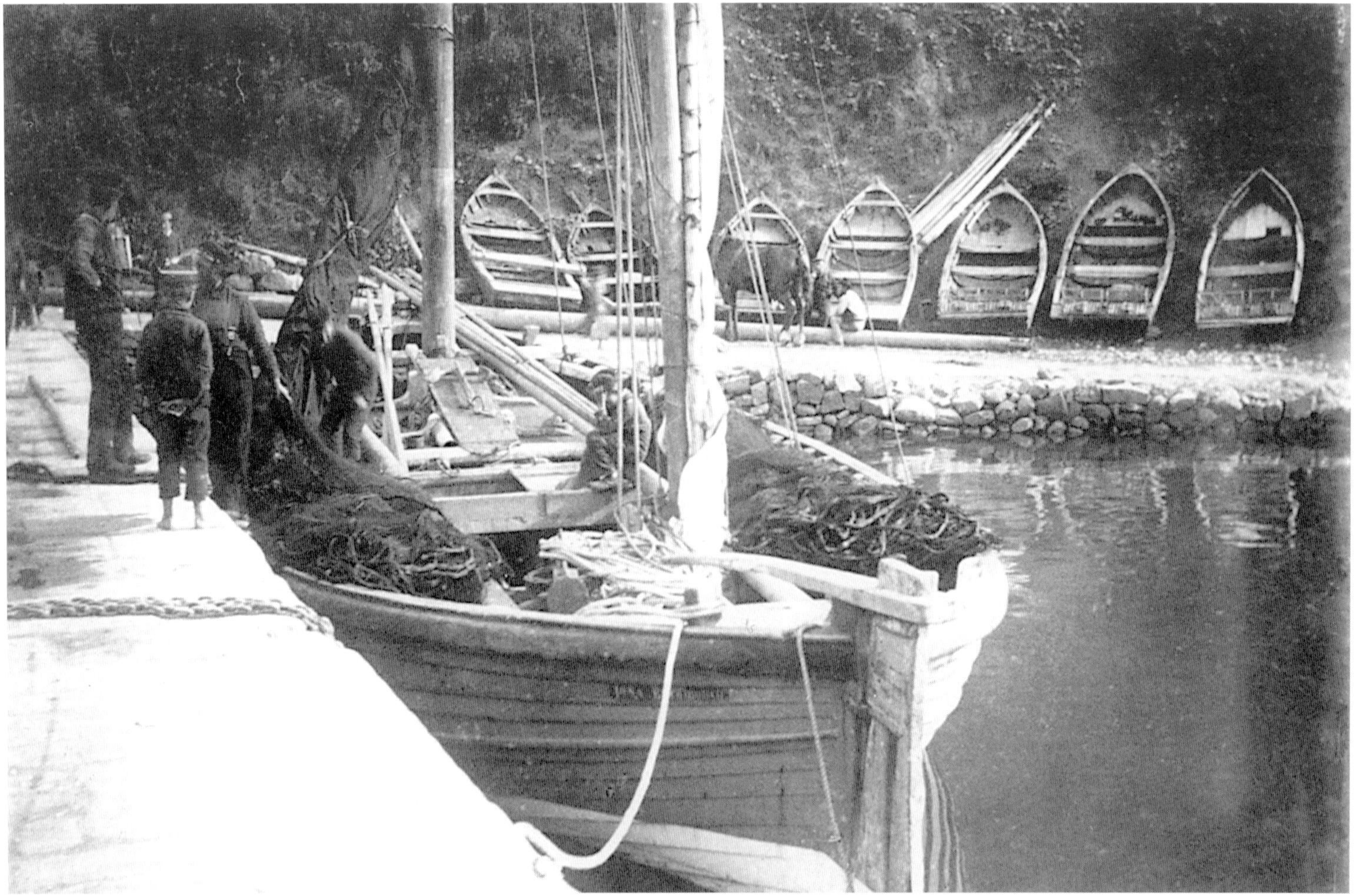

In the corner of the harbour, at the bottom of the Brae, the *Jane Elizabeth* of Burnmouth is getting ready for the next day's fishing. The barefoot lad is watching the heavy hemp ropes and nets being loaded onto the herring boat. Clearly a very early photograph, Weatherhead's new concept of closed-in decks with a holding area or 'hold' for the catch below had not been installed into the boat. Her long oars are lying in readiness to the starboard side of the vessel and her carved tiller sits in readiness for steering the boat out of the narrow confines of the harbour. Lobster and salmon punts are lying against the banking, allowing the rain water to wash the boats down and drain out the bottom.

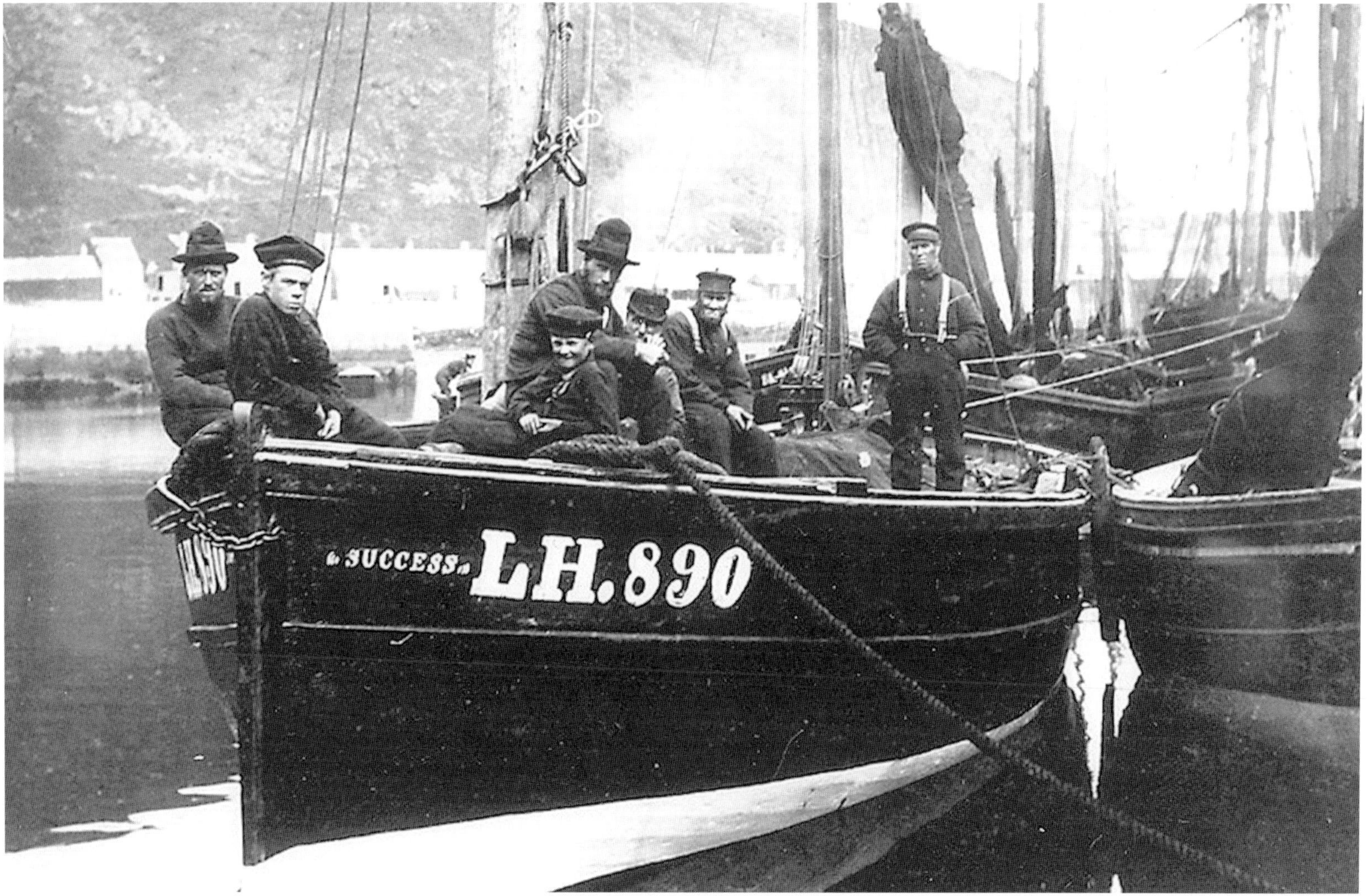

This is rather a poignant photograph as it is from before the 1881 Disaster. The Burnmouth fishing vessel LH.890 *Success*, registered in Leith, was one of the craft caught up in that treacherous maelstrom, although all of her crew survived that day. Three other fishing boats and two cobbles were lost with a total of 24 men drowned; some just within arms' reach of the shore. Note the difference in all the hats. A fisherman was certainly not dressed without his hat.

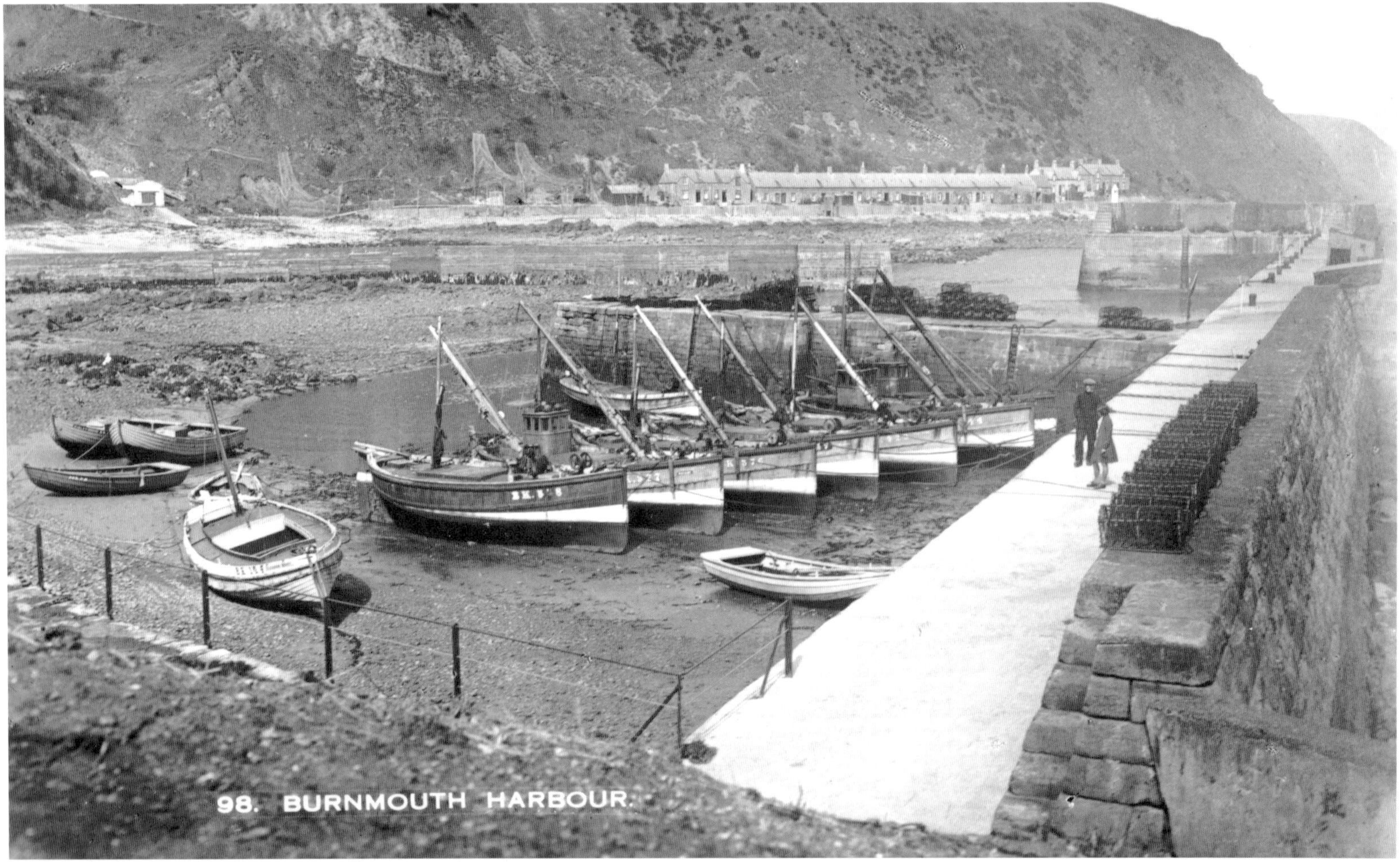

A splendid view of the newly inproved harbour, but with a complete change in the style of fishing boats. Seen here, high and dry, three of the craft have an even more radical design which includes a small 'wheelhouse' with closed-in decks, a sealed hatch into the hold and diesel engines. Smaller in size than the old herring fleet, these boats were much more economical and could venture further out to sea to where the fishing grounds were richer. Now, there are no herring barrels in evidence, just a line of lobster pots sitting on top of the harbour wall. There are still a few distinctively shaped punts which were used for salmon fishing as well as for tending to the inshore lobster pots. Long stretches of nets can be seen drying out up the hill behind Partanhall.

These two photographs were reproduced from old glass plates which had been found in a friend's attic. Clearly the photograph has been staged for the photographer, as in fact they are exactly the same view, but with the expertise of the photographer and telephoto lens two commercial views from the one scene have been made. The larger (wide-angle) view shows all of Cowdrait cottages with their pan tile roofs and smoking chimneys. There was little peat in this area of the Borders and interestingly there are a number of offshore open coal seams. Coal could be collected on the foreshore after particularly heavy storms, as well as driftwood. Coal was also imported into the village on the same ships which took the herring out.

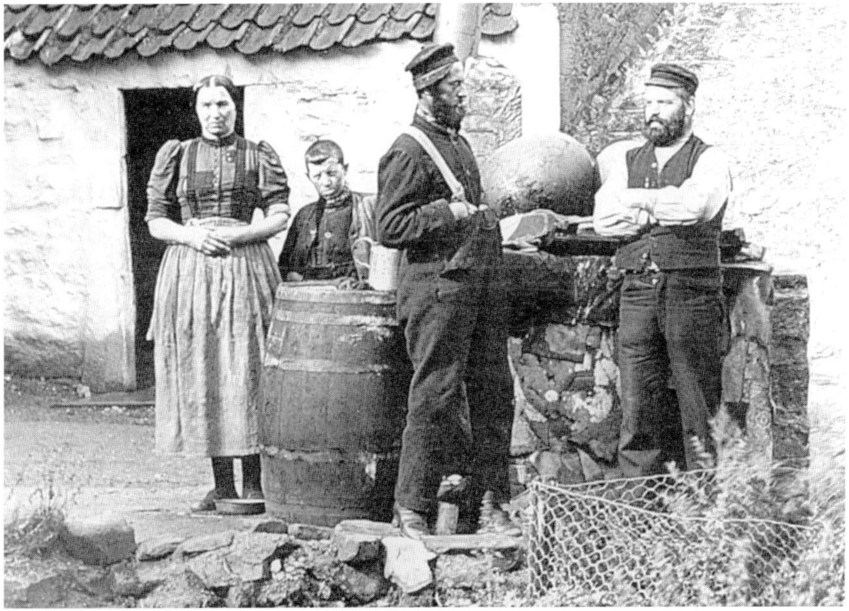

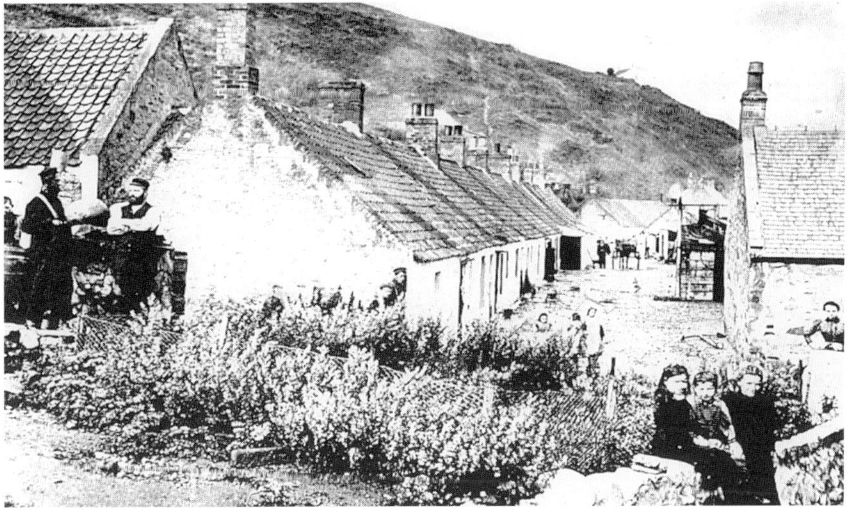

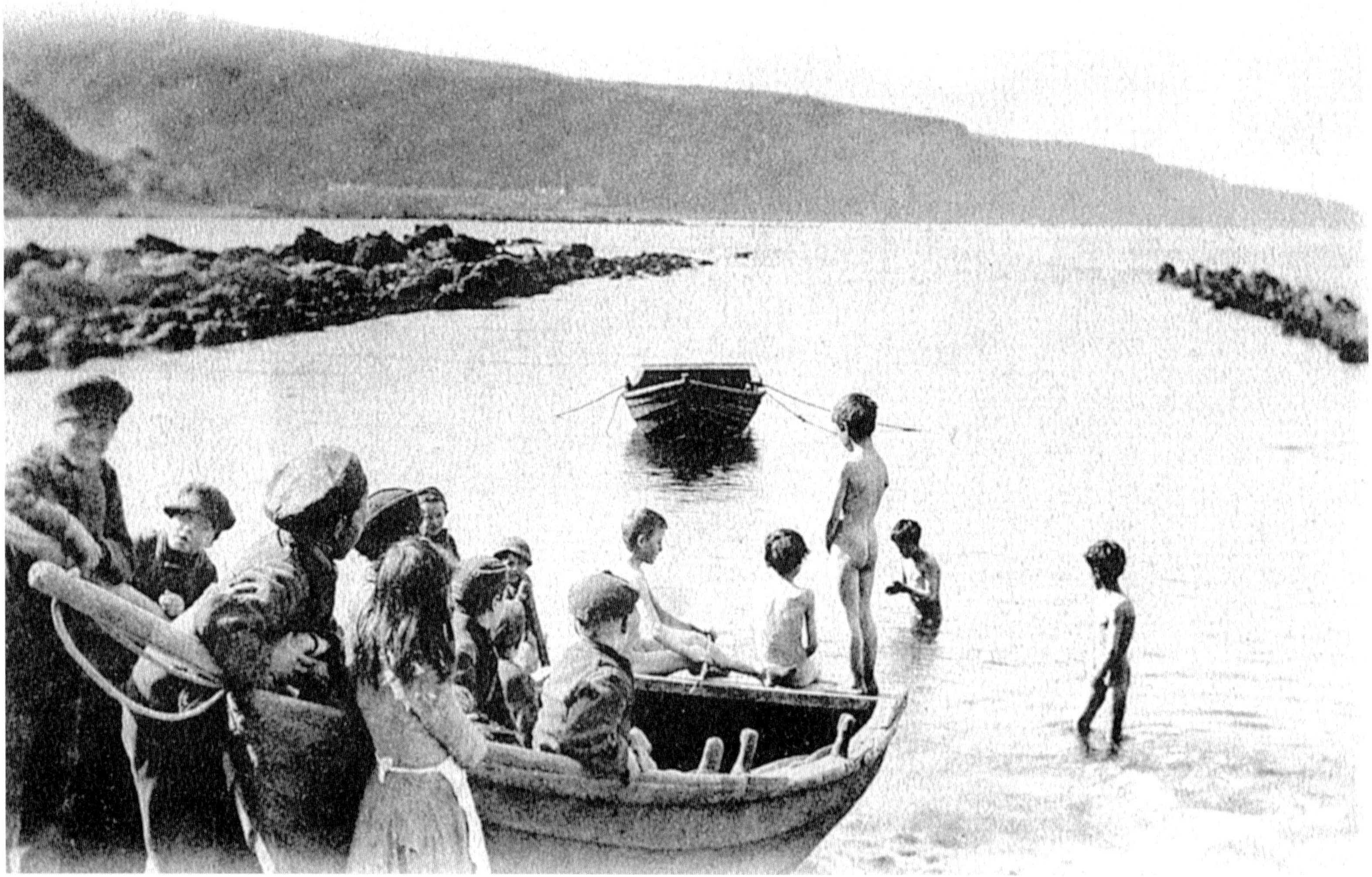

Whilst the postcard by Wane & Co. of Edinburgh does not indicate that the scene is at Burnmouth, we are able to recognize the distinctive shape of the sea cliffs and the village of Partanhall in the background at the foot of the Gorge. The design of the rowing 'punt' and the 'Raikie-step' hats are another indicator of this incredibly scenic coastal village. The geological rows of rocks on the foreshore are the final indicator for Lower Burnmouth.

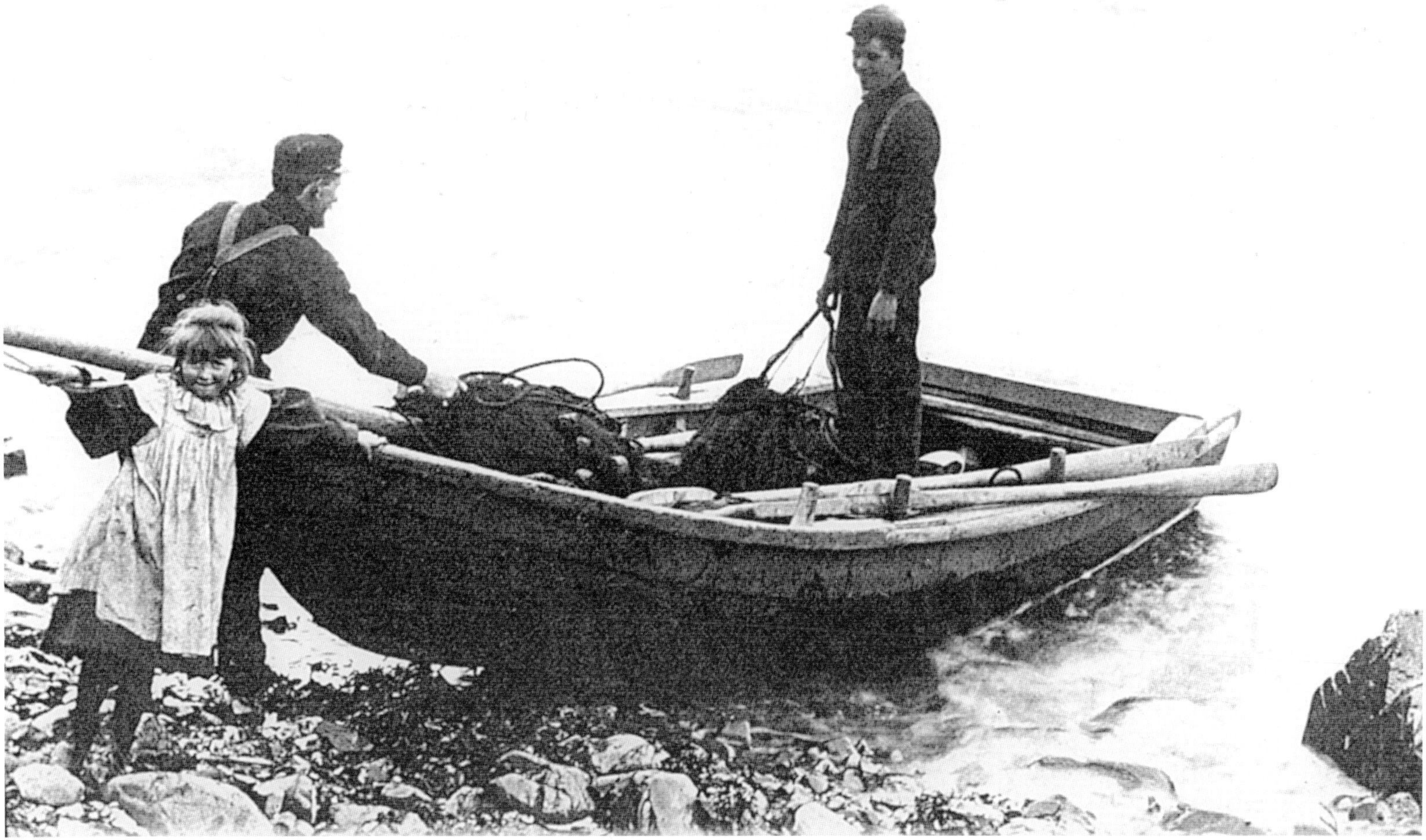

Again, here is the distinctive 'punt' used for long-lining and with a very shallow draught the fishermen could negotiate the shallow passages around the rocks to collect their crab and lobster craves. The boats have four sets of oars and rowlocks and a steeply raked, wide bow to keep the passengers dry and cut through the waves with ease. The child with her dross and smock will probably be one of the fishermen's daughters, asked to pose alongside the punt for added interest.

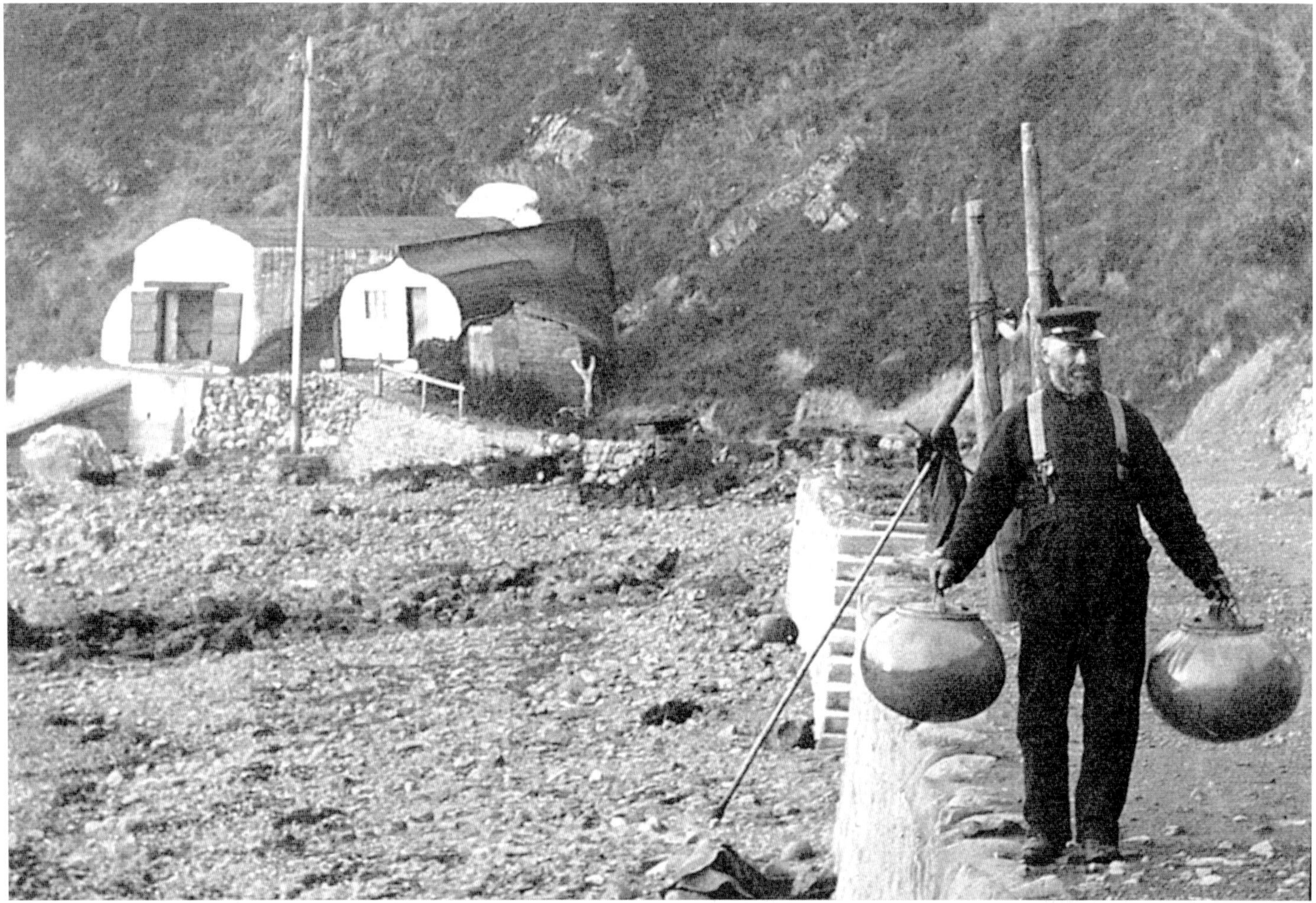

Walking from the harbour towards Partanhall is one of the local fishermen carrying a pair of pig bladder floats which were used to keep the heavy hemp ropes and nets afloat. The pig or ox bladders were so watertight, that they were actually used to store fresh water too. From the looks of the way this fisherman is walking, and the shape of the floats, these are probably filled with fresh water from the fresh water spring which comes down to the beach behind the upturned boat. In the background are the old coastguard shed and a small house made from an upturned boat and a smaller shed built with the remains of the boat. The only place in the vicinity which still has upturned boats as storage sheds is on Lindisfarne or Holy Island, south of Berwick-upon-Tweed.

Back cover: The lads and lassies in one of the herring yards along Eyemouth Harbour. Clearly they have been working as a number are covered in fish guts and shining silver scales. A carthorse with a loaded cart of creels of fish is in the background, probably brought directly from the beach to keep them very busy for a few more hours yet. The herring were gutted and salted and packed into barrels ready for sale and export. Whilst this view is clearly taken at the turn of the century, much of the herring were originally shipped to the Baltic States, Russia and the Caribbean to feed the slave population before Emancipation in 1827.

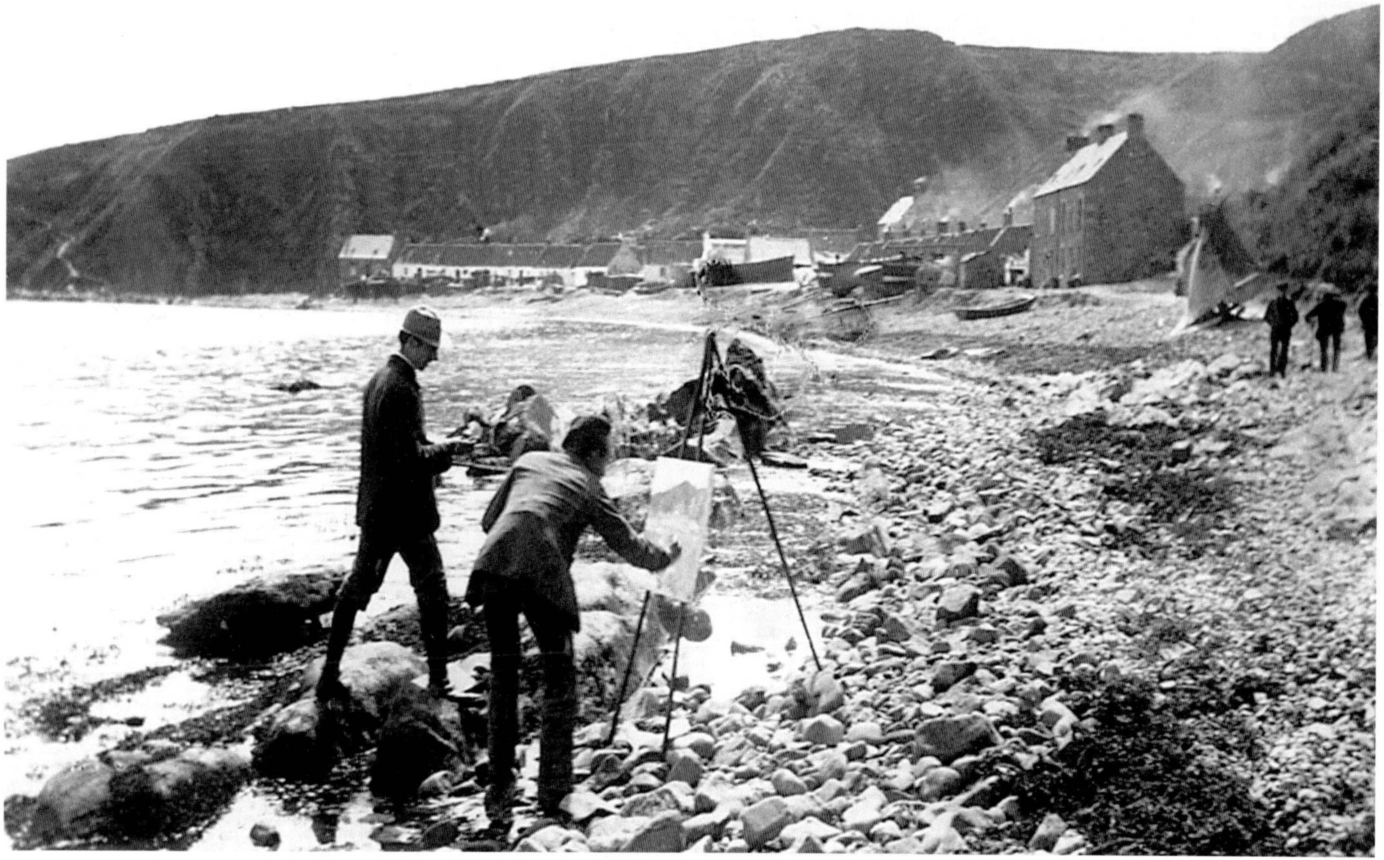

Burnmouth was so scenically beautiful that droves of artists and photographers visited the community and virtually every aspect of their daily lives was recorded. There is even a very fine collection of specific photographs held in the archives of the Greenwich Maritime Museum in London. Here the artists are depicting Cowdrait and Ross with the local fishermen in the foreground and the smaller fishing boats pulled up onto the foreshore between the houses.

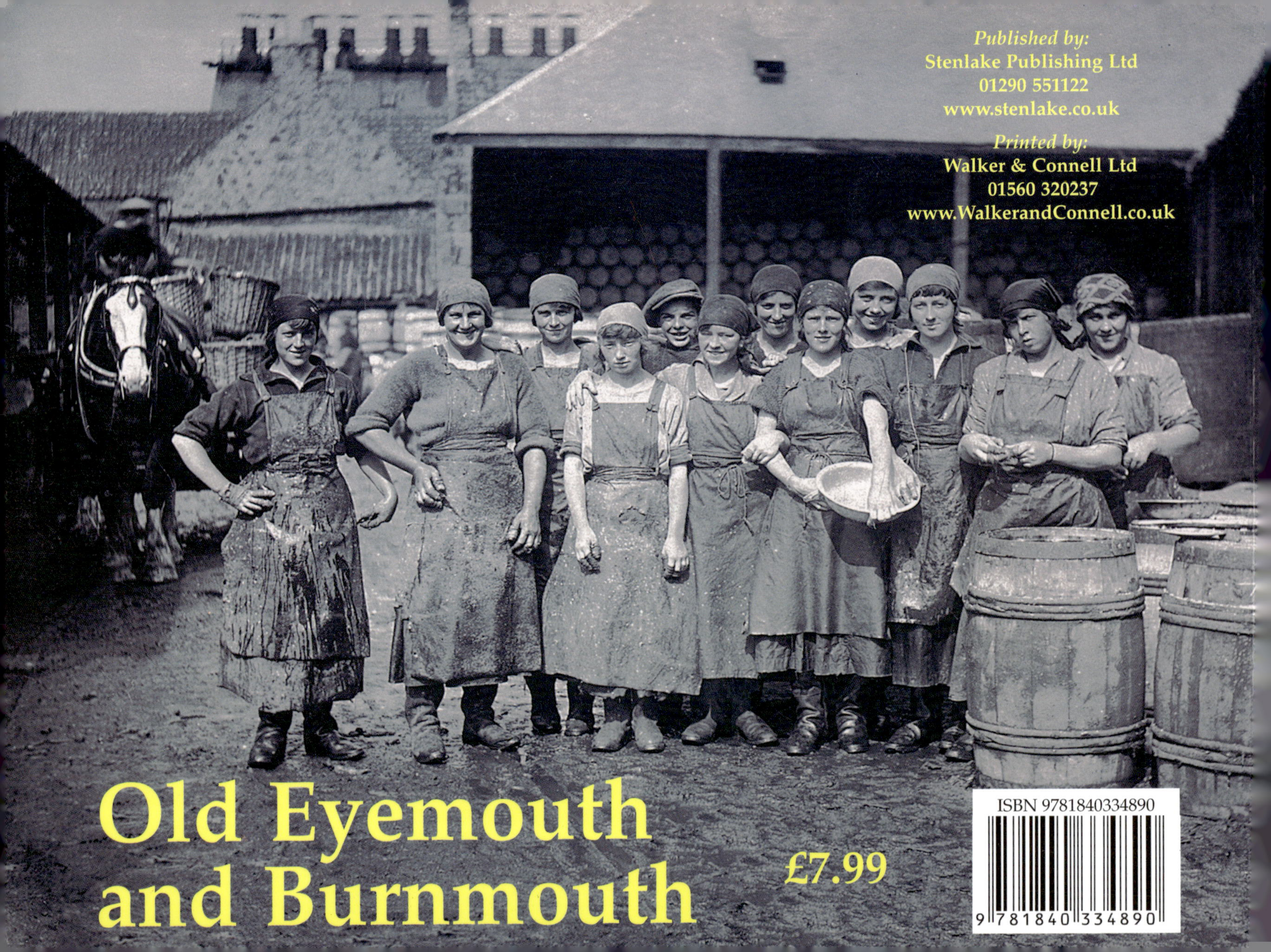

Published by:
Stenlake Publishing Ltd
01290 551122
www.stenlake.co.uk

Printed by:
Walker & Connell Ltd
01560 320237
www.WalkerandConnell.co.uk

Old Eyemouth and Burnmouth

£7.99

ISBN 9781840334890

9 781840 334890